Touring the
Washington D.C.
Area
by Bicycle

🚲 🚲 🚲

Peter Powers

Terragraphics

Eugene, Oregon

For Peg,
who has always believed in our venture.

Acknowledgements

The routes that are detailed in this book were suggested by a group of women and men who have thoroughly explored the roads and trails around Washington. Our thanks to Joanna Pistenmaa, Ted and Pat Beverley, Marcos Pernia, Margaret Lacy, Ada Rivera and Martha Penso for their help.

Edited by Melissa Carlson

Cover photo by James Blank/West Stock

TERRAGRAPHICS
P.O. Box 1025
Eugene, Oregon 97440

Library of Congress Cataloging-in-Publication Data
Powers, Peter.
Touring the Washington DC Area by Bicycle / Peter
  Powers, Renée Travis.
      p.   cm.
ISBN 0-944376-07-X
1. Bicycle touring--Washington Region--Guide books.
    2. Cycling paths--Washington Region--Guide books.
    3. Washington Region--Description and travel--Guide
books. I. Travis, Renée II. Title.
GV1045.5.W18P69   1991   91-9520
796.64'09753--dc20   CIP

Manufactured in the United States of America
First Printing, 1991
1   2   3   4   5   6   7   8   9   0

Contents

(cont.)

Introduction

It just *seems* that the ever-expanding metropolitan area has consumed all the good bike riding around the nation's capital. Actually, many miles of bike trails and country roads are within easy reach of the area's residents and visitors. You'll find that some of the rides in this book are close by, some you'll have to drive an hour or more to start, and some lend themselves better to a weekend get-away.

The Washington area has an active biking community, and a growing network of bike trails and designated routes. The Arlington bike trail system and the W&OD Regional Trail are good examples of first-class, off-road bike paths that are giving the Washington area a "biker-friendly" reputation. The routes in this book are mostly oriented to riding on paved roads, but a few of them use portions of different bike trails. In the section titled "Around the D.C. Area" you'll find a full description of several bike trails in the region.

Your choice of topography for rides around D.C. is practically unlimited. From the perfectly flat landscape of the eastern shore of Chesapeake Bay, to the choppy hills of northern Maryland, to the long climbs onto the Appalachian ridgeline, you can pick a ride that matches your skill and energy level. If you are looking for an 'easy' ride, most of the off-road bike trails are quite flat, and an out-and-back trip can be tailored to fit your time and ability constraints. They also offer the best picnic opportunities. The rides close to Chesapeake Bay also tend to be flat, and the Easton area, especially, is favored by those who want to avoid a hill-climb.

However, if a hill-climb or two is appealing to you, consider some of those rides that tackle the foothills of the Appalachians — or even Skyline Dr. itself. One note of caution, though, is to avoid

Skyline Dr. in the fall when the leaves are turning color. Motorists have their eyes and attention on the foliage, putting cyclists at an extra risk along this narrow and winding route.

Between mountain and bay you'll find the rolling farmlands of Virginia's horse country, the Potomac River Valley, Maryland's working farm country, and much more.

The focus of this book is its set of maps. They are as complete as they are unique. Touring, whether by foot or bicycle, throws us into an intimate relationship with the topography of a chosen route. Hills can become mountains and grades can seem to go on forever when you are under your own power. What looks like a winding country road on a typical map may actually be a series of switchbacks that climb up and over yet another ridge separating you from your destination! The 3D maps developed for this book provide you with a true representation of the landscape. The mileage log and route profile complete the picture of the ride ahead. They won't make it any easier to grind up and over those hills, but they will definitely take some of the unknown, and worry, out of your trip.

Along with the maps in this book, you'll find some general information pertinent to bicycle touring in this area. Other books cover any one of these topics in great detail. It is especially important that you become informed about fitness, with an emphasis on developing a good understanding of your capabilities and needs. Touring should be fun and fulfilling — not an unpleasant chore!

This book was designed to be taken with you as you venture around urban areas and into the countryside. The compact size is manageable for pocket or pack, and the layout will facilitate the navigation of each route.

Happy touring!

Pete Powers

Using this Book

The addition of the third dimension to the maps in this book sets them apart from other recreation maps. The computer generated view of the earth's surface provides valuable and clear information about the topography of an area you are planning to tour on bicycle. These 3D views accurately portray the nature of the landscape and the road system that covers it. Combined with the road map, route profile, route log and description, they provide you with a complete picture of many of the routes to explore in this region.

The area mapped

A good portion of the area around Washington, D.C. is covered by the maps in this book. The 31 routes that are profiled in the 16 map sets are mostly loops, reaching from Frederick County in Maryland, to Madison County in Virginia, to the East Bay of the Chesapeake. They include a wide range of lengths and topography, providing the opportunity for everyone to pick a route for their ability and interest.

About the maps

While each individual map covers only a portion of the area, the entire book presents you with a picture of the whole region. Each map highlights one or two ways to navigate around a specific area. Use of the profile to evaluate hilliness and length of a route allows you to estimate how long it will take to complete it. The 3D map and road map provide the information you need to pick an alternate route, or to shorten the one profiled.

The road maps are all oriented with north straight up, while the 3D maps rotate north to get the most complete view of the routes. Be aware that the scale of each map varies depending on the extent of the area being displayed.

(continued on page 12)

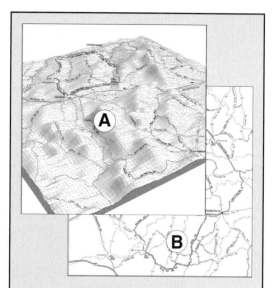

Map elements

A **3D map.** This map shows the topography of the area and highlights the selected route. It includes most of the roads and features shown on the road map, including the area's alternate bike routes.

B **Road map.** This is the traditional "planimetric" map showing the route and significant roads, towns, water, geographic features, and map symbols. The mileposts along the route, as well as "direction of travel" arrows, are shown.

C **Route profile.** This provides a cross-sectional view of each route. Elevation lines are labeled on both left and right sides, and mileage references are indicated along the bottom. Identifiable features are located along the route to help you see where you are.

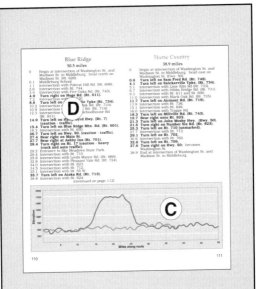

D **Route logs.** This is a complete set of directions for navigating through each route. It is especially useful in weaving your way through congested urban areas. Each log shows the accumulated distance travelled between turns and identifiable intersections and landmarks.

Index map. *(Title page of map set).* This small map locates the area covered by the larger maps on the following pages. It is accompanied by a general description of the area covered by the ride.

Calorie counter. *(End page of map set).* This shows estimates for calories burned for cycling the mapped routes. Total calories expended over the entire loop are estimated for various average cycling speeds; the estimate doesn't take hills into account.

The route profiles are displayed in a way that lets you easily compare them to each other. Don't be alarmed that some of them look more like a trip across the Himalaya mountains than Washington area topography — the vertical scale is exaggerated so that more of the "up and down" detail shows. Your first couple of rides will let your eyes and legs reach an understanding of how steep those hills really are!

There are two sets of profiles — with different exaggeration along the vertical axis. The profiles for routes close to Chesapeake bay, which are quite flat, are set against a blue background, and have a greater exaggeration in elevation. This brings out the small changes in topography that would be lost if they were displayed with the same vertical scale as the routes that venture into the Appalachian foothills.

Liability disclaimer

The goal of this publication from Terragraphics is to provide the most accurate and useful maps possible for Washington area cyclists. The routes displayed on these maps were compiled from a variety of sources, including city, county and state agencies and area cyclists. They are identified as being better suited for bicycle travel for safety, aesthetic or convenience reasons. Terragraphics assumes no liability for bicyclists travelling on these suggested routes. The maps are intended to aid in the selection of routes, but do not guarantee safety upon these roads. As with cycling on any road or trail, the cyclist assumes a risk while riding these suggested routes.

Resources

One of the attractive aspects of cycling as a participant sport is the convenience of being able to engage in it at will, be it alone or with company. However, at times you may wish for more information, or for more structure, or more diversity for your bike touring. The maps in this book provide you with enough information to plan and enjoy many different rides. It is always advisable to carry along a map that has a complete inventory of streets, especially in the more urban areas. If deciding where to go on your next ride calls for more information for exploring unfamiliar territory, some of the following resources may help you with your planning. This is definitely not a comprehensive list, and one of the best sources of information is always the folks at a bike shop in the area where you plan to cycle.

Maps

1. *Specific to bicycling.*

    ADC's Washington Area Bike Map. Metropolitan Washington Council of Governments. *Shows roads and trails suitable for biking in the D.C. region.* (202) 962-3200

    Getting Around Washington By Bicycle. D.C. Dept. of Public Works. *Set of eight maps for D.C. showing the suitability of city streets for cycling, as well as bike trails and routes.* (202) 727-5090

    Arlington County Bikeway Map. Arlington Co. Dept. of Public Works. *On- and off-road bike routes in Arlington, including several loop tours.* (703) 558-2941

    Baltimore Area Bike Map. Baltimore Regional Planning Council. *Recommended bike routes in Baltimore and central Maryland.* (301) 554-5600

    Lower Montgomery County Bicycle Route Map. Montgomery Co. Dept. of Transportation. *On- and off-road bikeways and other suggested routes.* (301) 217-2145

Maryland Bicycle Touring. State of Maryland Office of Tourism and Development. *Suggested bike routes and twelve loop rides in the State.* (800) 543-1036

The Kent County Bicycle Tour. Kent Co. Chamber of Commerce. *Nine loop rides, including map and mileage log, in Kent County, Md.* (301) 778-0416

Carroll County Bicycle Tours. Carroll Co. Tourism Office. *Ten maps, with mileage logs, for loop tours in "Bicycle Friendly" Carroll County, Md.* (301) 848-1388

Washington County Bicycle Tours. Washington Co. Tourism. *Ten maps, with mileage logs, for Frederick County, Md.* (301) 791-3130

Frederick County Bicycle Tours. Tourism Council of Frederick Co., Inc. *Nine loop tours and mileage logs for Frederick County, Md.* (301) 663-8687

Trail Guide to W&OD Regional Park. Northern Virginia Regional Park Authority. *Detailed strip map of the bike trail.* (703) 352-5900

Alexandria Recreational Facilities and Bike Trails Map. City of Alexandria. *Bike routes in the city.* (703) 838-4343

2. *General street maps.*

Rand McNally county and city maps.

American Automobile Association county and city maps (members only).

ADC Street Map Books. Atlas format by county for most Virginia and Maryland counties around D.C. (800) ADC-MAPS

3. *Topographic maps.*

USGS topographic maps. U.S. Dept. of the Interior. Various scales and level of detail. The 1:100,000 series is useful for planning rides of 20-100 miles.

Books

1. **Greater Washington Area Bicycle Atlas.** Washington Area Bicyclist Assoc. and Potomac Area Council, AYH.
2. **Bicycling Dorchester County.** Cycleways Publications.
3. **Bicycling Talbot County.** Cycleways Publications.
4. **Bicycling Central and Southern Maryland.** Cycleways Publications.
5. **Bicycling Northern Virginia.** Cycleways Publications.

Clubs and organizations

The following groups include recreation oriented, on-road cycling in their activities. There are other groups in the D.C area that focus on off-road riding, racing and training, and advocating for bicycle issues.

1. **Washington Area Bicyclist Association.**
   1015 31st. NW, Washington, D.C. 20007
   (202) 944-8567
2. **Potomac Pedalers Touring Club.**
   P.O.Box 23601, L'Enfant Plaza Sta.,
   Wash. D.C. 20026   (202) 363-TOUR
3. **Reston Bicycle Club**. P.O.Box 3389, Reston,
   VA 22090   (703) 860-0112
4. **Annapolis Bicycle Club.** P.O.Box 224,
   Annapolis, MD 21404   (415) 759-1205
5. **Baltimore Bicycling Club.** (301) 484-0306
6. **Frederick Pedalers.** P.O.Box 1293, Frederick,
   MD 21701
7. **Oxen Hill Bicycle & Trail Club.** P.O.Box 81,
   Oxen Hill, MD 20745
8. **Arlington County Bike Club.** c/o Arlington Co.
   Parks Dept., 300 N. Park Dr., Arlington, VA
   22203

General information

Information useful to D.C. area cyclists, and to those visiting from outside the region, is available from the following sources.   Each State/District Bike Coordinator can provide you with a list of resources for cyclists in their jurisdiction.   These lists are good starting points for finding detailed information about an area of interest, or about cycling activities that might appeal to you.   Maryland, especially, seems to be promoting bicycling - both on the State and County level.

Maryland

Maryland Department of Transportation
Bicycle Information Center
(301) 333-1663 and (800) 252-8776

Publications:
• Bicycling in Maryland: A Quick Reference Guide to Bicycle Information in Maryland.
• A Safety Handbook for Bicycle and Moped Owners.
• The Maryland Vehicle Law Pertaining to Bicycles.

- Bicycles: Prohibited on Expressways, Toll Facilities, and certain other Controlled Access Highways.
- Bicycle Access to Toll Bridges.
- Ferry Service in Maryland.
- Biking Trails of Special Interest.
- Undersized and Overlooked: A Motorist's Guide to Bicycle Safety.
- A Consumer's Guide to Bicycle Helmets.
- Tips for Safe Bicycling (for children).
- Specialized Bicycle Dealers/Repair Shops (a list).

District of Columbia

District of Columbia Dept. of Public Works
Bike Coordinator
(202) 939-8016

Publications:
- Bicycling in the District of Columbia Metro Area.
- Changing Modes (a newsletter).
- Bicycle Regulations.
- Bicycle Touring in the D.C. Metropolitan Area (a resource for touring cyclists visiting the area).
- Bicyclist's Survival Guide.
- Metro Bike Guide.

Virginia

Virginia Department of Transportation
State Bicycle Coordinator
(804) 786-2964

Publications:
- Bicycling on Virginia Roads; Laws and Safety Tips.
- Virginia...a Great Place to Bike (fact sheet).

National Park Service

National Park Service
Division of Public Information
(202) 619-7222

Publications:
- Maps of Rock Creek Park, C&O Canal and the Mount Vernon Trail.

Map Legend

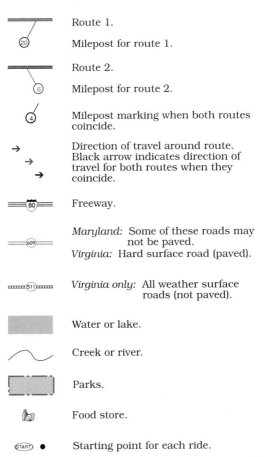

Route 1.

Milepost for route 1.

Route 2.

Milepost for route 2.

Milepost marking when both routes coincide.

Direction of travel around route. Black arrow indicates direction of travel for both routes when they coincide.

Freeway.

Maryland: Some of these roads may not be paved.
Virginia: Hard surface road (paved).

Virginia only: All weather surface roads (not paved).

Water or lake.

Creek or river.

Parks.

Food store.

Starting point for each ride.

Madison   Small town or community.

Manassas   Larger town or city.

Shenandoah NP Maps

ㅠ   Picnic area.

▲   Campground.

●   Developed facility (named on map).

━━━━━   Scenic overlook pull-out area.

Map Scale

The scale of each map varies according to the amount of land covered. Refer to the scale bar to estimate distances on the street map. The 3D map is presented in perspective view — i.e., the scale gets smaller from front to back. The route profiles are displayed in a common scale in order to allow easier comparisons among all routes in the book.

Map Orientation

Each of the road maps is oriented with north pointing towards the top of the page. The 3D maps are presented from either a southeast or southwest point of view. The north arrow on each map indicates its orientation. The 3D maps are rotated and scaled to provide the best possible view of the routes being profiled, and of some of the surrounding terrain.

Maryland
and
Virginia
Index Maps

There are great bicycling areas throughout the United States. The maps in this book will help you find and negotiate some of the best ones in and around Washington D.C. The two maps on the following pages allow you to locate rides in an area of particular interest. The numbered boxes on these index maps are keyed to the numbers on the route maps throughout the book and in the table of contents. The route maps contain detailed information about specific loop rides, and also show other roads that are good for cycling.

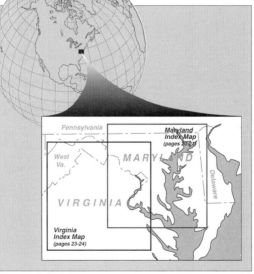

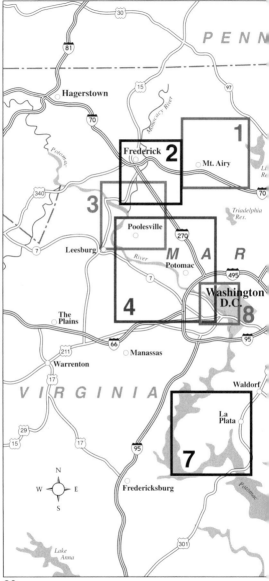

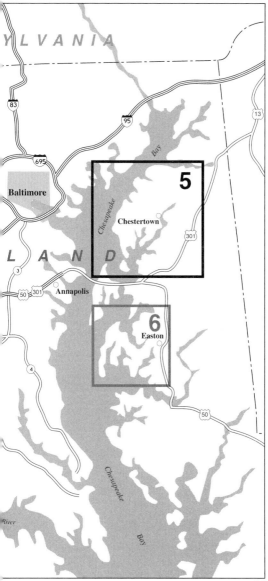

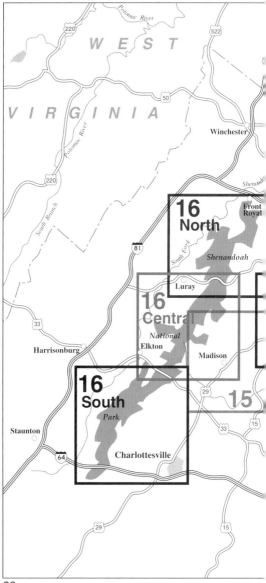

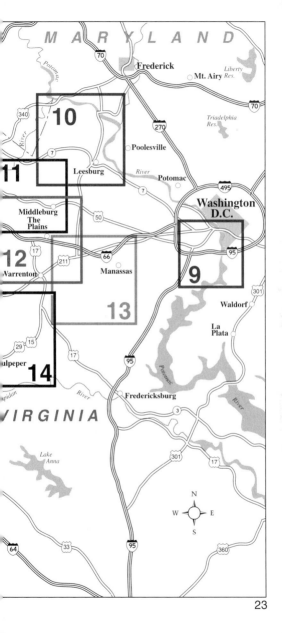

MARYLAND

70 Frederick
○ Mt. Airy Liberty Res.

340

10

70

River

270

Triadelphia Res.

7 ○ Poolesville

11

Leesburg

River

Potomac ○

495

7

Washington D.C.

Middleburg
The Plains

50

12

17

211

66

○ Manassas

95

9

301

Warrenton

13

Waldorf

La Plata

29 15

17

Culpeper

14

Fredericksburg

River

VIRGINIA

Potomac

River

95

3

301

17

Lake Anna

N
W ⊕ E
S

64

33

95

360

ROUTE SUMMARY

Mount Airy
Piney Run
and
Mt. Airy

Mt. Airy, the starting point for these rides, is nestled in the short, steep hills east of Frederick. Both routes wind their way through this hilly and mostly rural countryside, flattening out occasionally along a ridge or valley bottom. Piney Run Park is a good bet for a picnic along the Piney Run loop. There are picnic areas, a nature center and paddle-boat and canoe rentals available. Carroll and Frederick Counties are both promoting cycle touring, and additional route information can be obtained from their Visitor Information Centers.

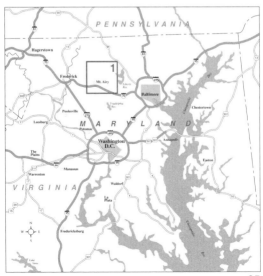

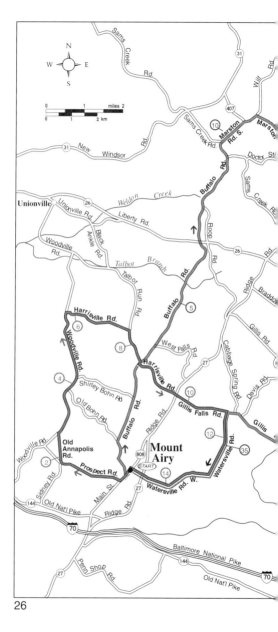

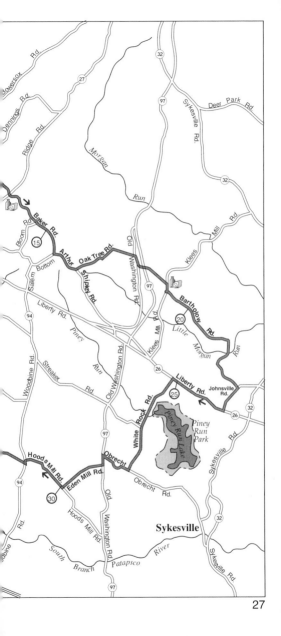

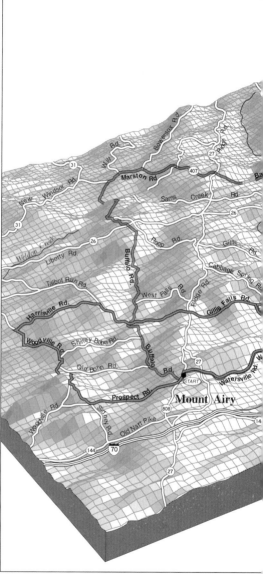

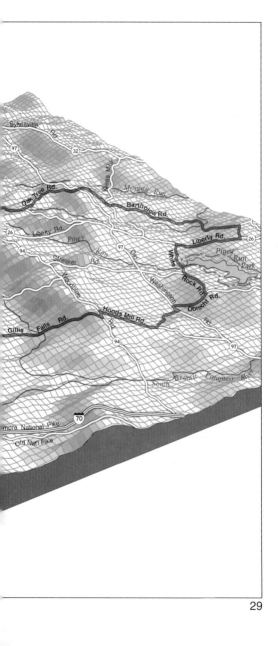

Piney Run

38.3 miles

0	Begin at Mt. Airy Elementary School on N. Main St. in Mt. Airy; head south on N. Main St.
0.2	**Turn right on Buffalo Rd.**
1.1	Intersection with Old Bohn Rd.
2.3	Intersection with Shirley Bohn Rd.
3.2	Intersection with Harrisville Rd.
3.3	**Turn right at stop sign to stay on Buffalo Rd.**
3.8	Intersection with West Falls Rd.
5.3	Intersection with Black Ankle Rd.
6.8	Intersection with Liberty Rd. (Rt. 26).
7.7	Intersection with Roop Rd.
7.9	Intersection with Hooper Delight Rd.
9.2	**Turn left on Sams Cr. Rd.**
9.6	**Turn right on Marston Rd. S.**
10.5	**Turn right on Marston Rd. (Rt. 407).**
11.4	Intersection with Bowersox Rd.
12.3	Intersection with Doctor Stitley Rd.
12.5	Intersection with Dennings Rd.
13.4	Intersection with Ridge Rd. (Rt. 27); continue straight onto Baker Rd.
14.5	Intersection with Bloom Rd.
15.2	**Bear right onto Salem Bottom Rd.**
15.6	**Turn left on Arthur Shipley Rd.**
16.2	**Turn left on Oak Tree Rd.**
17.4	**Turn right on Bear Branch Rd.**
18.0	**Turn right on Old Washington Rd.**
18.2	**Turn left on Bartholow Rd. (unmarked).**
18.4	Intersection with Rt. 97.
19.1	**Turn right on Klees Mill Rd.**
19.3	**Turn left on Bartholow Rd.**
20.9	Intersection with Linton Rd.
22.5	Intersection with Gibbons Rd.
23.0	**Turn right on Johnsville Rd.**
23.6	**Turn right on Liberty Rd. (Rt. 26).**
25.1	**Turn left on White Rock Rd.**
26.6	Intersection with Streaker Rd.

(cont.)

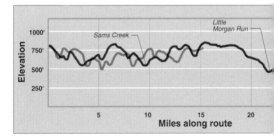

Mt. Airy

15.3 miles

Begin at the Mt. Airy Elementary School on
N. Main St. in Mt. Airy; head south on N.
Main St.

.3	**Turn right on Prospect Rd.**
.9	**Turn right on Old Annapolis Rd.**
.6	**Turn right on Woodville Rd.**
.1	Intersection with Mattie Haines Rd.
.2	Intersection with Shirley Bohn Rd.
.7	Intersection with Glissans Mill Rd.
.8	**Turn right on Harrisville Rd.**
.7	**Turn right to stay on Harrisville Rd. at intersection with Talbot Run Rd.**
.4	**Turn right on Buffalo Rd.; then left to get back on Harrisville Rd.**
.8	**Turn right on Ridge Rd. (Rt. 27); then immediate left on Gillis Falls Rd.**
0.8	Intersection with Runkles Rd.
1.3	**Turn right on Watersville Rd.**
3.0	**Turn right on Watersville Rd. W.**
3.5	Intersection with Runkles Rd.
4.8	Intersection with Ridge Rd. (Rt. 27).
5.2	**Turn left on N. Main St.**
5.3	End at Mt. Airy Elementary School.

Piney Run (cont.)

7.0	Intersection with Martz Rd.; entrance to Piney Run Park.
7.7	**Turn right on Obrecht Rd.**
8.6	**Turn left on Rt. 97.**
8.8	**Turn right on Eden Mill Rd.**
0.0	**Turn right on Hoods Mill Rd.**
1.2	**Turn left on Woodbine Rd. (Rt. 94).**
1.3	**Turn right on Gillis Falls Rd.**
4.3	**Turn left on Watersville Rd.**
6.0	**Turn right on Watersville Rd. W.**
7.8	Intersection with Ridge Rd. (Rt. 27).
8.2	**Turn left on N. Main St.**
8.3	End at Mt. Airy Elementary School.

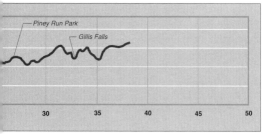

Calorie Counter

Piney Run: 38.3 miles

Average Speed (mph)	Riding Time	Calories Expended*
5	7 hrs. 40 mins.	1010
10	3 hrs. 50 mins.	1310
15	2 hrs. 33 mins.	1530
20	1 hr. 55 mins.	2090

Mt. Airy: 15.3 miles

Average Speed (mph)	Riding Time	Calories Expended*
5	3 hrs. 04 mins.	420
10	1 hr. 32 mins.	450
15	1 hr. 01 mins.	550
20	46 mins.	810

* Estimations from tractive-resistance calculations
Whitt and Wilson, "Bicycling Science"

Frederick
Lily Pons
and
New Market

Both of these rides make a quick exit from downtown Frederick into the surrounding farmland. The route through New Market just as quickly climbs into the hills to the east of the city, and winds its way through a mixture of dairy farm and forest land. The second route stays in the valley as it stretches south toward Sugarloaf Mtn. There are plenty of alternate routes for extending or varying this route — many of them lacing the valley floor. Lily Pons makes an interesting stop along the way, offering a look at a wide variety of aquatic plants and a good bird-watching spot.

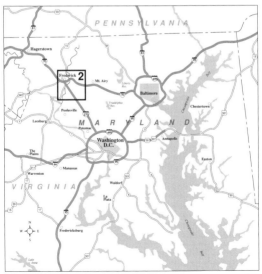

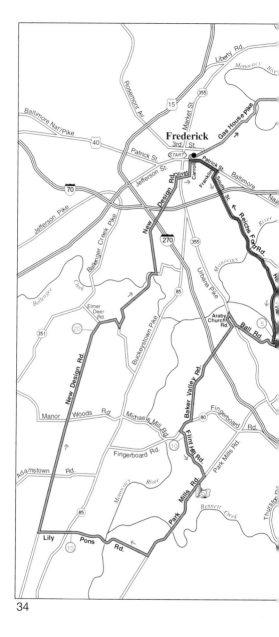

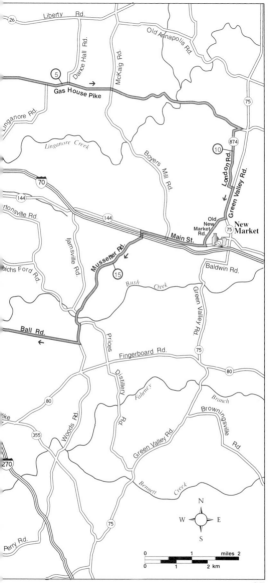

Lily Pons
25.8 miles

0	Begin at the Visitor's Center on Church St. between Market St. and Carroll St.; head east on Church St.
0.2	**Turn right on East St.**
0.3	**Turn left on Patrick St. (Rt. 144).**
1.0	**Turn right on Franklin St.**
1.2	**Turn left on South St.**
1.5	Cross under I-70 (caution - truck traffic), becomes Reichs Ford Rd.
2.9	Cross Monocacy River.
3.2	Intersection with Pinecliff Park Rd.; entrance to Pinecliff Park; picnic area.
3.4	**Turn right on Reels Mill Rd.**
5.0	Cross RR tracks and single lane bridge.
5.4	**Turn right on Ball Rd.**
6.5	**Turn right on Urbana Pike (Rt. 355).**
6.8	**Turn left on Araby Church Rd.**
7.3	**Turn right on Baker Valley Rd.**
7.9	Cross under I-270.
9.5	**Turn right on Fingerboard Rd. (Rt. 80).**
9.8	**Turn left on Flint Hill Rd.**
11.0	**Turn right on Park Mills Rd.**
12.1	Intersection with Mt. Ephraim Rd.
13.2	**Turn right on Lily Pons Rd.**
13.8	Entrance to Lily Pons Gardens.
14.2	Cross Monocacy River.
15.1	Intersection with Buckeystown Pike (Rt. 85); becomes Oland Rd.
15.8	**Turn right on New Design Rd.**
17.0	Intersection with Adamstown Rd.
18.4	Intersection with Manor Woods Rd.
20.6	**Bear right where Elmer Derr Rd. intersects with New Design Rd.**
21.1	**Turn left to stay on New Design Rd.**
23.2	Intersection with Ladd Lane.
23.5	Intersection with Crestwood Blvd.
23.8	Cross over I-270.
24.1	Cross over I-70.
24.8	**Turn left on Market St.; then immediate right on Mt. Olivet Blvd.**
25.0	**Turn left on Carroll St.**
25.4	**Turn left on All Saints St.**
25.5	**Turn right on Market St.**
25.8	**Turn right on Church St.;** end at the Visitor's Center.

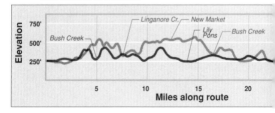

New Market

25.0 miles

.0   Begin at the Visitor's Center on Church St. between Market St. and Carroll St.; head east on Church St.

.2   Bear left to continue on Church St.; becomes Gas House Pike.

.2   Cross Monocacy River.

.4   Intersection with Linganore Rd.

.0   Intersection with McKaig Rd.

.4   Turn right (at stop sign) on London Rd.

0.7   Turn left on Crickenberger Rd.; then right on Green Valley Rd. (Rt. 75).

1.6   Turn right on Old New Market Rd.

2.4   Turn right on Main St. (Rt. 144) in New Market.

3.3   Intersection with Boyers Mill Rd.

3.9   Turn left on Mussetter Rd.

6.4   Cross RR tracks (caution); **then turn left on Ijamsville Rd.**

7.1   Turn right on Ball Rd.

.9.7   Turn right on Reels Mill Rd.

21.7   Turn left on Reichs Ford Rd.

21.9   Pinecliff Park Rd., entrance to Pinecliff Park; picnic area.

23.6   Cross underneath I-70 (caution - watch for truck traffic).

23.9   Turn right on Franklin St.

24.1   Turn left on E. Patrick St. (Rt. 144).

24.9   Turn right on Carroll St.

25.0   Turn right on Church St.; end at the Visitor's Center.

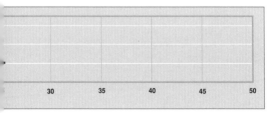

Notes:

_____

_____

_____

_____

_____

_____

_____

_____

_____

_____

_____

_____

_____

_____

_____

_____

_____

_____

Calorie Counter

Lily Pons: 25.8 miles

Average Speed (mph)	Riding Time	Calories Expended*
5	5 hrs. 10 mins.	710
10	2 hrs. 35 mins.	780
15	1 hr. 43 mins.	930
20	1 hr. 17 mins.	1350

New Market: 25.0 miles

Average Speed (mph)	Riding Time	Calories Expended*
5	5 hrs.	690
10	2 hrs. 30 mins.	760
15	1 hr. 40 mins.	910
20	1 hr. 15 mins.	1320

* Estimations from tractive-resistance calculations
Whitt and Wilson, "Bicycling Science"

Poolesville

Poolesville
and
Sugarloaf Mtn.

Sugarloaf Mountain dominates the landscape in this area, and pops into view regularly along both of these routes. The side trip up the mountain is a little strenuous, but is also rewarded with good views to both the east and west. There are hiking trails in Sugarloaf Mtn. Park, and one that leaves from the west parking lot leads to the top of the mountain. There is a nice variety of scenery and vegetation along the roads in this area — from open farmland to enclosed wooded canopy. This is a rural area, and the roads are generally narrow and winding, with a low volume of traffic. Route 28 carries more traffic than other roads in the area.

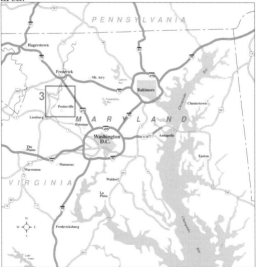

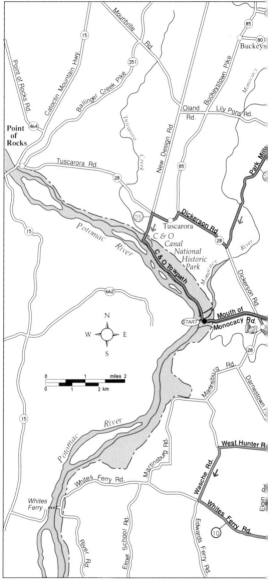

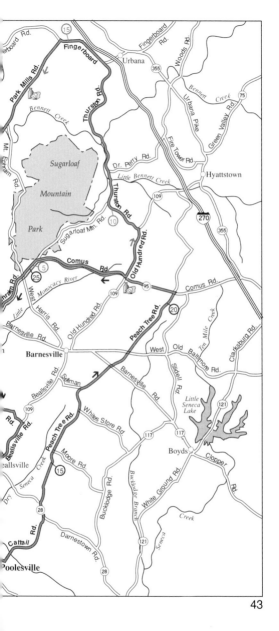

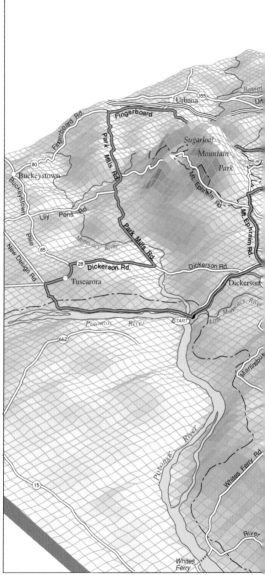

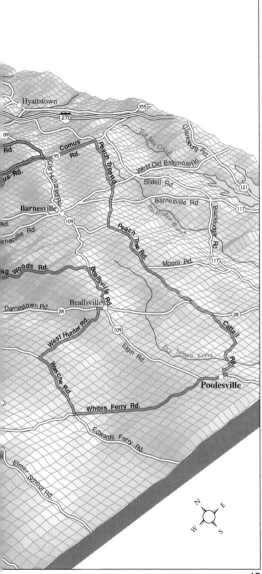

Poolesville

29.6 miles

0   Begin at the Mouth of the Monocacy Aqueduct Park on the C&O Canal. *(Follow signs to the aqueduct to the beginning point - picnic area).* Head east on Mouth of Monocacy Rd.

0.3   Cross railroad tracks (caution).

1.4   Turn right on Dickerson Rd.

1.7   Turn left on Big Woods Rd. just after crossing under the RR tracks.

4.3   Turn right on Beallsville Rd.

5.6   Turn right on Darnestown Rd. (Rt. 28), then immediate left on West Hunter Rd.

7.3   Turn left on Wasche Rd.

8.8   Turn left on Whites Ferry Rd.

10.9 Intersection with West Willard Rd.

11.0 Intersection with Elgin Rd.

11.4 Turn left on Cattail Rd.

13.0 Intersection with Cattail Lane.

13.5 Turn left on Darnestown Rd. (Rt. 28).

13.7 Turn right on Peach Tree Rd.

15.2 Intersection with Moore Rd.

16.4 Intersection with Whites Store Rd.

16.9 Intersection with Sellman Rd.; **bear right to stay on Peach Tree Rd.**

17.9 Intersection with Barnesville Rd.

18.4 Intersection with West Old Baltimore Rd.

20.4 Turn left on Comus Rd.

21.8 Intersection with Old Hundred Rd. (Rt. 109).

22.7 Intersection with Barley Field Rd.

24.3 Bear left on Mount Ephraim Rd.

25.3 Entrance to Sugarloaf Mountain Park.

25.8 Intersection with West Harris Rd.

27.2 Intersection with Barnesville Rd.

27.8 Turn right on Mouth of Monocacy Rd.

28.2 Intersection with Dickerson Rd.

29.3 Cross railroad tracks (caution).

29.6 End at Mouth of Monocacy Aqueduct.

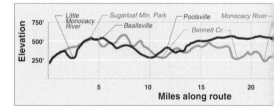

Sugarloaf Mtn.

27.8 miles

Begin at the Mouth of the Monocacy Aqueduct Park on the C&O Canal. *(Follow signs to the aqueduct to the beginning point - picnic area).* Head east on Mouth of Monocacy Rd.

.3	Cross RR tracks (caution).
.4	Intersection with Dickerson Rd.
.8	**Turn left on Mt. Ephraim Rd.**
.4	Intersection with Barnesville Rd.
.8	Intersection with W. Harris Rd.
.3	Entrance to Sugarloaf Mountain Park; 2.6 mile alternate route up Sugarloaf Mtn. to good views east & west (picnic areas, toilets).
.3	**Bear right onto Comus Rd.**
.9	Intersection with Barley Field Rd.
.8	**Turn left on Old Hundred Rd. (Rt. 109).**
.0	**Turn left on Thurston Rd.**
0.2	Intersection with Sugarloaf Mtn. Rd.
0.8	Intersection with Covell Rd.
2.6	Intersection with Peters Rd.
4.2	Continue straight onto Fingerboard Rd. (Rt. 80).
4.7	Intersection with Roderick Rd.
5.5	**Turn left on Park Mills Rd.**
6.8	Intersection with Flint Hill Rd.
7.4	Intersection with Peters Rd.
8.1	Intersection with Mt. Ephraim Rd.
9.1	Intersection with Lily Pons Rd.
9.8	Intersection with Ira Sears Rd.
1.6	Intersection with Page Rd.
2.4	**Turn right on Dickerson Rd. (Rt. 28)** (caution - fast moving traffic).
3.4	Intersection with Greenfield Rd.
4.0	**Turn left to stay on Rt. 28; follow signs to "Point of Rocks".**
4.4	**Bear right to stay on Rt. 28 in Tuscarora.**
4.9	**Turn left on New Design Rd.**
5.6	Enter Nolans Ferry Park.
5.8	**Turn left into first parking pull-out to join C&O Canal Trail (picnic, toilets).**
7.8	End at Monocacy Aqueduct.

Sugarloaf Mtn. Park

C&O Canal Trail

| 30 | 35 | 40 | 45 | 50 |

Notes:

Calorie Counter

Poolesville: 29.6 miles

Average Speed (mph)	Riding Time	Calories Expended*
5	5 hrs. 55 mins.	820
10	2 hrs. 58 mins.	890
15	1 hr. 58 mins.	1060
20	1 hr. 29 mins.	1550

Sugarloaf Mtn.: 27.8 miles

Average Speed (mph)	Riding Time	Calories Expended*
5	5 hrs. 34 mins.	760
10	2 hrs. 47 mins.	840
15	1 hr. 51 mins.	990
20	1 hr. 23 mins.	1450

* Estimations from tractive-resistance calculations
Whitt and Wilson, "Bicycling Science"

Potomac
C&O Canal
and
Lake Needwood

The community of Potomac lies right at the fringe of the more dense Washington suburbs, and these two rides reflect this urban to rural transition. The Lake Needwood loop takes you through some residential and commercial areas before and after a very pleasant ride on the Rock Creek bike path. This path extends south all the way into the District and can connect with the Rock Creek loop (map 8). The C&O loop explores a more rural part of Montgomery County before joining with the C&O Canal National Historic Park. The Canal path can be muddy and slick after a rain — ride carefully!

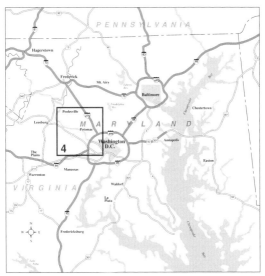

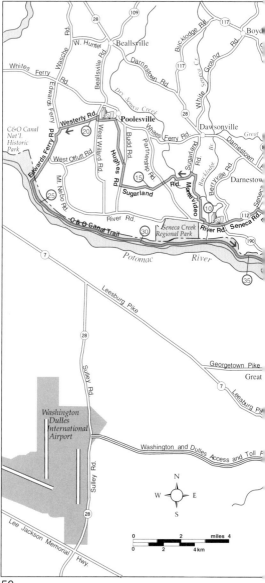

50

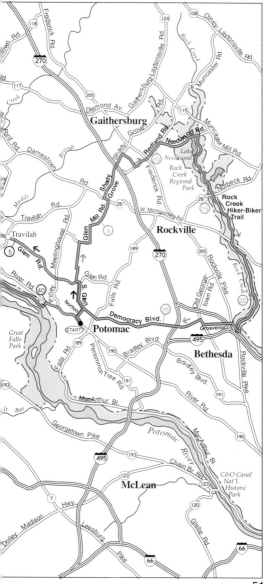

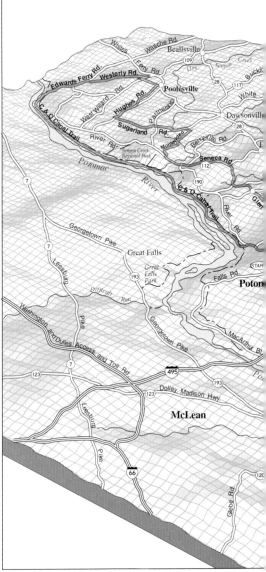

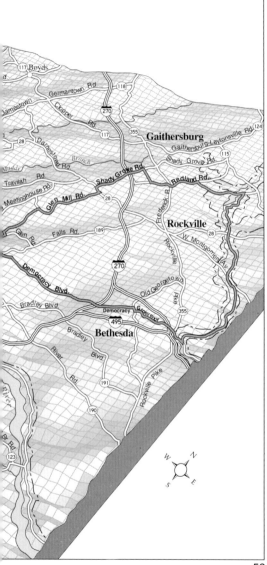

C&O Canal
41.8 miles

0	Begin at Potomac Elementary School on River Rd. just north of Potomac; head north on River Rd. (There is a bike path on the right side of the road)
0.5	**Turn right on Norton Rd.**
1.1	**Turn left on S. Glen Rd.**
2.2	Intersection with Glen Rd.; keep to the left, cross the bridge, then left to stay on Glen Rd.
3.2	Intersection with Piney Meetinghouse Rd.
5.4	Intersection with Travilah Rd.
6.2	**Bear left onto Query Mill Rd.**
6.8	**Turn right on Esworthy Rd.**
8.2	**Turn left on Seneca Rd. (Rt 112) where Esworthy Rd. splits.** (Caution - faster moving traffic.)
9.7	Intersection with River Rd. (Rt. 190).
10.5	**Turn right on Old River Rd. just after bridge.**
10.8	**Turn right on Montevideo Rd.**
13.0	**Turn left on Sugarland Rd.**
14.2	Intersection with Partnership Rd.
14.8	**Bear right to stay on Sugarland Rd.**
16.1	**Turn right on Hughes Rd.**
18.8	**Turn left on Westerly Ave.**
19.5	**Turn right on West Willard Rd., then immediate left on Westerly Rd.**
21.0	**Turn left on Edwards Ferry Rd.**
22.4	Intersection with W. Offutt Rd.
23.4	**Turn left on River Rd.**
23.5	**Turn left onto C&O Canal Trail** (picnic area).
27.2	Sycamore landing.
31.6	Seneca Creek.
37.7	Swains Lock, **turn left on Swains Lock Rd.** (toilets, picnic area).
40.0	**Turn right on River Rd.** (Caution - heavy traffic.)
40.5	Intersection with Piney Meetinghouse Rd.
41.4	Intersection with Norton Rd. (There is a bike path on the left hand side of the road).
41.8	End at the Potomac Elementary School.

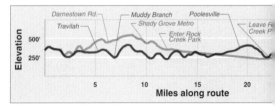

29.5 miles

)   Begin at Potomac Elementary School on River Rd. just north of Potomac; head north on River Rd. (There is a bike path on the right side of the road).

0.5   **Turn right on Norton Rd.**
1.1   **Turn left on S. Glen Rd.**
2.2   Intersection with Glen Rd.; keep to the left, cross the bridge, **then turn right on Glen Mill Rd.**
3.5   Intersection with White Clover Terrace.
3.9   **Bear right at intersection with Boswell Lane.**
5.1   Intersection with Ridge Dr.
5.4   Intersection with Viers Dr.
6.1   Intersection with Ritchie Pkwy.
6.2   **Turn left on Darnestown Rd.**
6.3   **Turn right on Shady Grove Rd.**
       (Caution - heavy traffic to Gather Rd.)
7.1   Intersection with Key West Ave.
7.6   Cross over I-270.
8.2   **Turn right on Gather Rd.**
8.9   **Turn left on Redland Rd.**
9.5   Intersection with Frederick Rd.
9.9   Shady Grove Metro station.
10.0   Intersection with Crabbs Branch Rd.
10.3   **Turn right on Needwood Rd.**
11.8   Cross Lake Needwood.
12.0   **Turn right on Beach Dr.** (Enter Rock Creek Regional Park; open sunrise to sunset; picnic areas.)
12.9   **Bear right onto one-way road.**
13.2   **Turn right into parking lot at bottom of loop; pick up bike trail heading south.**
15.1   Intersection with Norbeck Rd.
17.2   Intersection with Viers Mill Rd.
18.8   Intersection with Randolph Rd.
20.6   Intersection with Knowles Ave.
21.8   **Turn right on Beach Dr. cross over Rock Cr.**
22.1   **Turn left, follow sign for Grosvenor Lane, cross Rockville Pike.**

(continued on page 56)

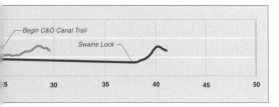

Lake Needwood (cont. from page 55)
22.4 Cross over I-270.
23.3 Turn left on Cheshire Dr., then immediate right on Old Georgetown Rd. (caution - heavy traffic to Seven Locks Rd.)
23.5 Turn left on Democracy Blvd.
24.8 Montgomery Mall.
25.6 Intersection with Seven Locks Rd.
27.9 Intersection with Falls Rd.; becomes S. Glen Rd.
28.5 Turn left on Norton Rd.
29.0 Turn left on River Rd.
29.5 End at Potomac Elementary School.

Notes:

Calorie Counter

C&O Canal: 41.8 miles

Average Speed (mph)	Riding Time	Calories Expended*
5	8 hrs. 22 mins.	1150
10	4 hrs. 11 mins.	1260
15	2 hrs. 47 mins.	1600
20	2 hrs. 05 mins.	2190

Lake Needwood.: 29.5 miles

Average Speed (mph)	Riding Time	Calories Expended*
5	5 hrs. 54 mins.	820
10	2 hrs. 57 mins.	880
15	1 hr. 58 mins.	1060
20	1 hr. 28 mins.	1540

* Estimations from tractive-resistance calculations
Whitt and Wilson, "Bicycling Science"

Chestertown
Betterton Beach
and
Rock Hall

Betterton calls itself the "jewel of the Chesapeake", and the cycling in this area sparkles as well. The Betterton Public Beach is an excellent destination for a picnic and a swim — though you'll need to pack your food with you. There are plenty of variations to these routes on the many country roads in the area, and it would be easy to fill a two- or three-day cycling weekend out of Chestertown. There is a little more texture to the landscape here than you'll find further south, and more of a sense of it being working farmland. You can find a good place to stay and a good meal in Chestertown.

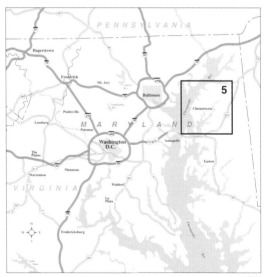

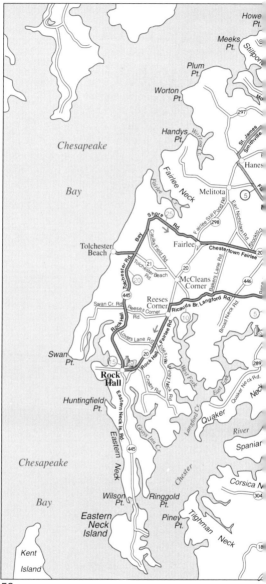

Howel Pt.

Meeks Pt.

Stillpon

Plum Pt.

Worton Pt.

297

St. James

Smithville

Handys Pt.

Hanes

Fairlee Neck

Melitota

5

Chesapeake

Shore 25

Fairlee Still Pond Rd.

298

Earl Nicholson Rd.

Stockson

Bay

Bay Shore Rd.

Caulks Field Rd.

Fairlee

Chestertown Fairlee

20

20

Tolchester Beach

Tolchester Beach Rd.

21

Tolchester Beach Rd.

445

McCleans Corner

Bakers Lane Rd.

446

Swan Cr. Rd.

Reeses Corner

Reeses Corner Rd.

Ricauds Br. Langford Rd.

10

Broad Neck Rd.

5

Rock Hall Rd.

Lovers Lane Rd.

Rock Hall Fairlee Rd.

20

West Fork

289

Swan Pt.

15

Rock Hall

Eddes Vly Rd.

Piney Neck Rd.

Crosby Rd.

Quaker Neck Rd.

Neck

Huntingfield Pt.

Eastern Neck Is. Rd.

Eastern Neck

445

Langford Cr.

East Fork

Quaker

River

Spaniar

Chesapeake

Long Ins Cr.

Chester

Corsica N

Bay

Wilson Pt.

Ringgold Pt.

Piney Pt.

Tighman Neck

304

Eastern Neck Island

18

Kent Island

58

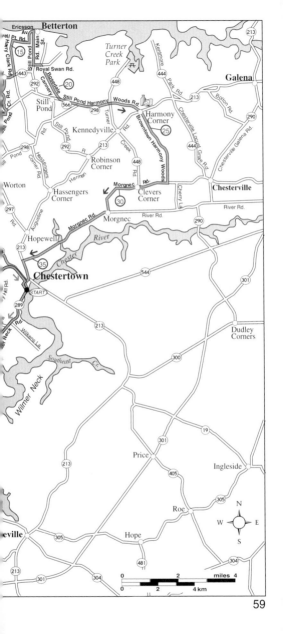

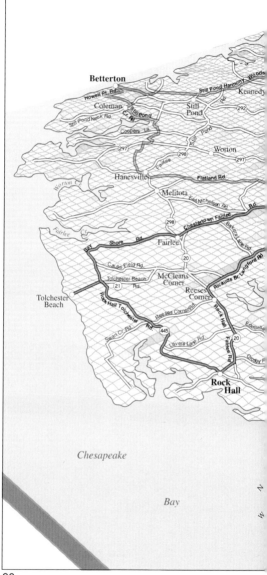

60

Betterton Beach

37.1 miles

0	Begin at Phillip Wilmer Park on the Chester River in Chestertown; **turn right on Rt. 289**; becomes Cross St.
0.3	**Turn left on Hight St.**
1.3	Intersection with Rt. 291.
1.5	**Turn right on Flatland Rd. (Rt. 514).**
3.5	**Turn right on Morris Rd.**
5.0	**Turn right on Porters Grove Worton Rd.**
5.2	Continue straight onto Porters Grove Hansville Rd. where Porters Grove Melitota Rd. bears left.
6.4	**Turn right on Rt. 298.**
6.6	**Turn left on St. James Newton Rd.**
6.9	**Turn right on St. James Smithville Rd.**
7.9	Intersection with Possum Hollow Rd.
9.1	**Turn right on Smithville Rd. (Rt. 297).**
9.4	**Turn left on Montabello Lake Rd.**
10.6	Intersection with Coopers Lane; continue straight onto Still Pond Cr. Rd.
11.7	Cross bridge and bear left where Bessicks Corner Rd. continues straight.
12.2	Intersection with Wymont Park Rd.
13.3	**Turn right on Still Pond Neck Rd.**
13.8	**Turn left on Clark Rd.**
15.4	**Turn right on Howell Point Rd.**
16.2	**Turn left on Erickson Ave.**
16.9	Betterton Public Beach; picnic, toilets, swimming; head south on Main St.
18.4	**Turn left on Royal Swan Rd.**
18.8	**Turn right on Rosedale Cannery Rd.**
20.4	**Bear left onto Maple St.**
20.7	Continue straight onto Still Pond Harmony Woods Rd. (Rt. 566) (unmarked).
21.5	**Bear left onto Rt. 298 at intersection with Bloomfield Rd.**
22.8	Intersection with Turner Creek Rd.
24.1	Intersection with Rt. 213.

(continued on page 64)

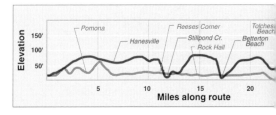

Rock Hall

33.8 miles

Begin at the Phillip Wilmer Park on the Chester River in Chestertown; head south on Rt. 289.

9	Intersection with Rt. 664.
.1	**Turn right on Langford Pomona Rd.**
.6	**Bear left to stay on Langford Pomona Rd. where Airy Hill Rd. continues straight.**
1	Intersection with Brices Mill Rd.
.6	Intersection with Broad Neck Rd. (Rt. 446); becomes Ricauds Branch Langford Rd.
.5	Intersection with Bakers Lane.
9	Intersection with Sandy Bottom Rd. (St. Paul's Episcopal Church on corner).
0.9	**Turn left on Rt. 20.**
1.4	Intersection with Reeses Corner Rd.
1.9	Intersection with Shipyard Lane.
2.9	Intersection with Lover's Lane Rd.
4.3	Intersection with Rt. 288.
4.9	**Turn right on Main St. (Rt. 445).**
6.5	Intersection with Humphreys Point Rd.
7.0	Intersection with Lover's Lane Rd.
8.2	Intersection with Reeses Comer Rd.
0.9	**Turn left on Rt. 21.**
1.9	**Turn around point at beach** (no facilities); head east on Rt. 21.
2.8	**Turn left on Bayshore Rd.**
4.0	Intersection with Caulks Field Rd.
5.5	Intersection with road to Fairlee Public Landing.
6.0	Intersection with Georgetown Rd.
7.1	**Turn right on Rt. 298 then immediate left.**
7.2	**Turn left on Chestertown Fairlee Rd.**
7.6	**Turn left on Rt. 20 North.**
8.8	Intersection with Bakers Lane.

(continued on page 64)

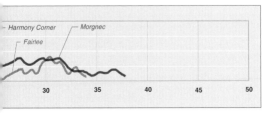

Betterton Beach *(continued from page 62)*

26.4 Intersection with Browntown Blacks
      Station Rd.
27.8 Turn right on Morgneck Rd.
29.2 Intersection with Kennedyville Morgneck Rd.
30.2 Intersection with Wallace Rd.
30.8 Intersection with Stryckning Rd.
31.3 Turn right on Rt. 291.
32.4 Intersection with Perkins Hill Rd.
33.8 Bridge over Morgneck Cr.
35.7 Turn left on Washington Ave. (Rt. 213).
36.6 Turn right on Spring Ave. (Rt. 289).
36.7 Turn left on High St.
36.8 Turn right on Cross St.
37.1 End at Phillip Wilmer Park.

Rock Hall (continued from page 63)

28.8 Intersection with Bakers Lane.
30.5 Intersection with Langford Rd. (Rt. 446).
31.3 Intersection with Brices Mill Rd.
31.8 Intersection with Airy Hill Rd.
32.4 Intersection with Rt. 514.
32.6 Intersection with Rt. 291.
33.4 Turn right on Cross St.
33.8 End at Phillip Wilmer Park.

* Note: Rt. 445 south goes to the Eastern
  Neck Island Wildlife Refuge where you can
  find hiking trails and wildlife observation
  areas. It is a 16.2 mile (round trip)
  extension to the route if you go all the
  way to Bogles Wharf landing.

Calorie Counter

Betterton Beach: 37.1 miles

Average Speed (mph)	Riding Time	Calories Expended*
5	7 hrs. 25 mins.	1050
10	3 hrs. 43 mins.	1170
15	2 hrs. 28 mins.	1480
20	1 hr. 51 mins.	2030

Rock Hall: 33.8 miles

Average Speed (mph)	Riding Time	Calories Expended*
5	6 hrs. 46 mins.	920
10	3 hrs. 23 mins.	1030
15	2 hrs. 15 mins.	1290
20	1 hr. 41 mins.	1780

* Estimations from tractive-resistance calculations
  Whitt and Wilson, "Bicycling Science"

Easton
Tilghman Island
and
Oxford

These routes explore an area of the east Bay that has long been a favorite of cyclists. Settlements date back to the 1600's, and the Oxford-Bellevue ferry has been operating since 1836. Although the terrain is flat, be prepared to be challenged by the wind and heat in the summer. Most of the roads have wide shoulders, and those that don't aren't heavily trafficked. Tilghman Island makes a great destination for lunch — either for a picnic or in a restaurant. The combination of great cycling, historic interest, fine food and good places to stay in this area makes an enjoyable weekend away from the city.

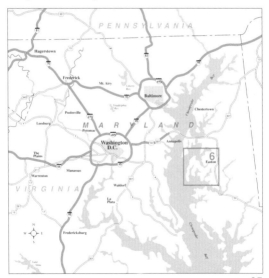

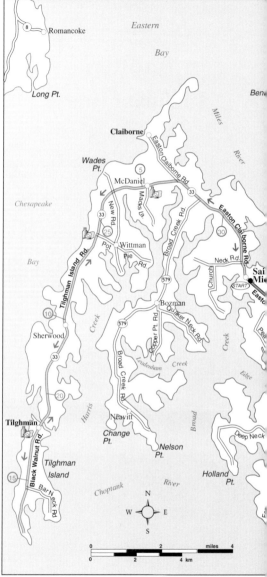

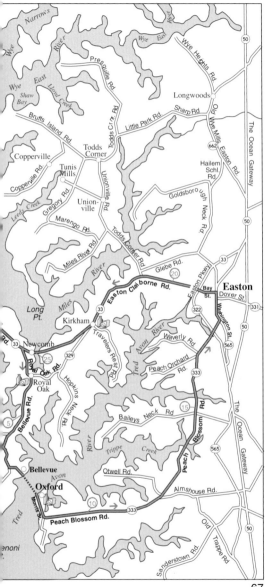

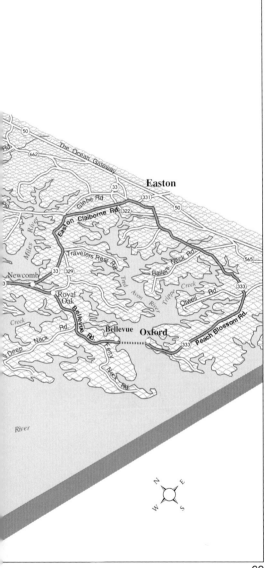

Tilghman Island
32.2 miles

0	Begin at St. Michaels Elementary School in St. Michaels; head west on Seymour Ave.
0.1	**Turn right on Talbot St. (Rt. 33); continue through town of St. Michaels.**
3.1	Intersection with Broad Cr. Rd. (Rt. 579).
3.8	**Bear left to stay on Rt. 33 where Rt. 451 continues straight.**
4.9	Intersection with Macks Lane.
7.5	Intersection with Bayshore Rd.
10.0	Intersection with Lowes Wharf Rd.
13.2	Cross bridge over Knapps Narrows onto Tilghman Island.
15.6	Intersection with Fairbank Rd.
16.1	**Turn around point; access to water; picnic spot;**

Note: Return along the same route to St. Michaels.

32.2 End at St. Michaels Elementary School.

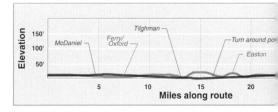

Oxford

27.8 miles

0	Begin at St. Michaels Elementary School in St. Michaels; head west on Seymour Ave.
0.1	**Turn left on Talbot St. (Rt. 33).**
0.7	Intersection with Lincoln Ave.
2.7	**Turn right on Royal Oak (Rt. 329).**
3.1	Intersection with Station Rd.
3.8	**Turn right on Bellevue Rd.;** follow sign to Bellevue Oxford Ferry (caution - narrow road with no shoulder).
5.3	Intersection with Goose Neck Rd.
5.6	Intersection with Deep Neck Rd.
6.6	**Bear left to stay on road to ferry.**
7.3	Ferry landing; picnic area; toilets Note: In Oxford there is public access to the water along the shore to the east of the ferry landing.
7.4	Continue straight after leaving the ferry landing.
7.6	Town park; picnic area.
8.0	**Bear left to stay on main road (Rt. 333);** becomes Peach Blossom Rd.
9.7	Intersection with Evergreen Rd.
10.2	Intersection with World Farm Rd.
11.6	Intersection with Almshouse Rd.
12.7	Intersection with Spring Rd.
14.3	Intersection with Bailey Rd.
16.1	Intersection with Cedar Pt. Rd.
16.9	Intersection with Easton Parkway (Rt. 322).
17.3	**Turn left on Washington St. (Rt. 565).**
18.0	Downtown Easton.
18.2	**Turn left on Bay St. (Rt. 33).**
18.7	Intersection with Easton Parkway (Rt. 322).
20.4	Intersection with Rt. 370.
21.1	Intersection with Doncaster Rd.
22.9	Intersection with West Rt. 329.
25.1	Intersection with East Rt. 329.
27.7	**Turn right on Seymour Ave.**
27.8	End at St. Michaels Elementary School.

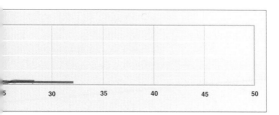

Notes:

___

Calorie Counter

Tilghman Island: 32.2 miles

Average Speed (mph)	Riding Time	Calories Expended*
5	6 hrs. 26 mins.	880
10	3 hrs. 13 mins.	980
15	2 hrs. 09 mins.	1230
20	1 hr. 37 mins.	1700

Oxford: 27.8 miles

Average Speed (mph)	Riding Time	Calories Expended*
5	5 hrs. 34 mins.	760
10	2 hrs. 47 mins.	840
15	1 hr. 51 mins.	990
20	1 hr. 23 mins.	1450

* Estimations from tractive-resistance calculations
Whitt and Wilson, "Bicycling Science"

Smallwood Park
Port Tobacco
and
Maryland Point

These two routes cover a very rural part of southern Maryland. You'll find rolling terrain, an occasional view of the Potomac River, and many historic markers about the Civil War and John Wilkes Boothe. On the Port Tobacco route the Saint Ignatius Catholic Church sits on a small hill and offers both a good view of the Port Tobacco River and a look at a church built in 1798. Throughout the area there are mostly low traffic volume roads with good pavement. The trip around Maryland Point is especially enjoyable, with lots of trees, an occasional swamp, and long straight stretches of gently rolling road.

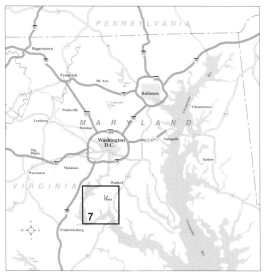

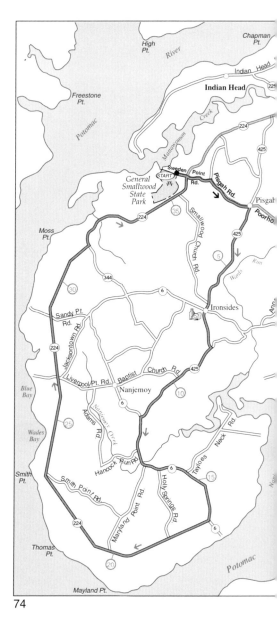

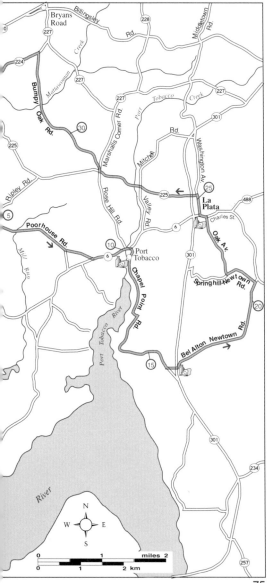

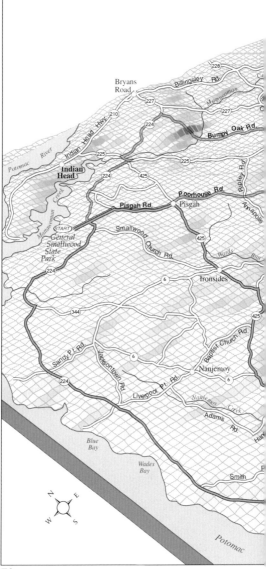

Port Tobacco

40.7 miles

0	Begin at the entrance to Smallwood State Park; head east on Sweden Pt. Rd.
0.3	Intersection with Rt. 224.
1.2	**Turn right on Bicknell Rd. (Pisgah Rd.)**
2.8	Intersection with Rt. 425; continue straight onto Poorhouse Rd.
3.4	Intersection with Stuckey Rd.
5.0	Intersection with Ripley Rd. and Annapolis Woods Rd.
8.7	**Turn left on Rt. 6.**
9.6	Intersection with Shirley Blvd.
10.1	Intersection with Rose Hill Rd.
10.4	**Turn right on Chapel Point Rd.**
10.7	Port Tobacco Historic site.
14.2	Entrance to Chapel Point State Park.
14.4	Saint Ignatias Catholic Church (c. 1798).
16.6	Intersection with Hwy. 301; continue straight onto Bel Alton-Newton Rd.
17.0	Intersection with Fairgrounds Rd.
17.5	Intersection with Dove Rd.
20.4	Intersection with White Stag Rd.
20.9	**Turn left on Spring Hill Newton Rd. just before Rt. 6.**
22.1	**Turn right on Oak Ave.**
23.8	**Turn right to stay on Oak St. where Patuxent Dr. continues straight.**
24.4	**Turn left on E. Charles St. in La Plata.**
24.6	**Turn right on Washington Ave.**
25.2	**Turn left on Hawthorne Dr.**
25.5	Intersection with Hwy. 301; continue straight onto Rt. 225.
27.4	Intersection with Mitchell Rd. & Valley Rd.
28.9	**Turn right on Marshall's Corner Rd. at intersection with Rose Hill Rd.; then immediate left on Bumpy Oak Rd.**
30.5	Intersection with Gwynn Rd.
32.8	Intersection with Ashland Dr.
33.6	**Turn left on Rt. 224.**
36.1	**Turn left to stay on Rt. 224 at intersection with Rt. 225.**
36.5	**Turn right to stay on Rt. 224.**

(cont.)

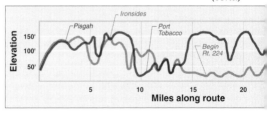

Maryland Point

36.5 miles

Begin at entrance to Smallwood State Park; head east on Sweden Pt. Rd.

3 Intersection with Rt. 224; continue on Sweden Pt. Rd.
.2 Turn right on Bicknell Rd.
.8 Turn right on Rt. 425.
5 Intersection with Smallwood Church Rd.
7 Intersection with Rt. 6; continue straight on Rt. 425.
1 Intersection with Durham Church Rd.; **bear right to stay on Rt. 425 (Ironsides Riverside Rd.).**
3 Intersection with Friendship Landing Rd.
7 Intersection with Baptist Church Rd.
1.5 Turn left on Rt. 6.
2.6 Intersection with Hancock Run Rd.
3.0 Cross Nanemjoy Cr.
3.1 Intersection with Maryland Pt. Rd.
3.6 Intersection with Holly Springs Rd.
4.6 Intersection with Tayloes Pt. Rd.
6.1 Intersection with Benny Gray Pt. Rd.
6.5 Turn right on Rt. 224.
0.1 Intersection with Maryland Pt. Rd.
3.6 Intersection with Smith Pt. Rd.
6.7 Intersection with Liverpool Pt. Rd.
8.7 Intersection with Sandy Pt. Rd.
1.5 Turn left to stay on Rt. 224 where Rt. 344 turns right.
4.4 Intersection with Stump Neck Rd.
5.5 Intersection with Smallwood Church Rd.
6.2 Turn left on Sweden Pt. Rd.
6.5 End at the entrance to Smallwood State Park.

***ort Tobacco** (continued)*
7.2 Lackey High School.
3.7 Intersection with Bicknell Rd.
9.0 Intersection with Creeds Mill Rd.
0.4 Turn right on Sweden Pt. Rd.
0.7 End at entrance to Smallwood State Park.

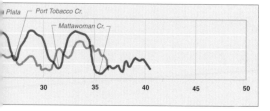

Notes:

Calorie Counter

Port Tobacco: 40.7 miles

Average Speed (mph)	Riding Time	Calories Expended*
5	8 hrs. 08 mins.	1120
10	4 hrs. 04 mins.	1230
15	2 hrs. 43 mins.	1560
20	2 hrs. 02 mins.	2140

Maryland Point: 36.5 miles

Average Speed (mph)	Riding Time	Calories Expended*
5	7 hrs. 18 mins.	1030
10	3 hrs. 39 mins.	1150
15	2 hrs. 26 mins.	1460
20	1 hr. 49 mins.	1990

* Estimations from tractive-resistance calculations
  Whitt and Wilson, "Bicycling Science"

Washington, D.C.
Rock Creek Park
and
National Monuments

These routes are rideable anytime, but are perhaps best enjoyed on the weekend. Beach Dr., from Broad Branch Rd. to the Maryland line is closed to autos from 7a.m. Sat. to 7p.m. Sun., and traffic downtown is greatly reduced. Rock Creek Park has always been somewhat of an oasis downtown, and with the road closure on weekends it becomes especially appealing to cyclists. The Rock Creek Trail extends from the Maryland/D.C. line to Lake Needwood (see Map 4). The Monuments route travels the length of the Mall, and places of interest are detailed on page 164. Bridge crossings are shown in detail on page 166.

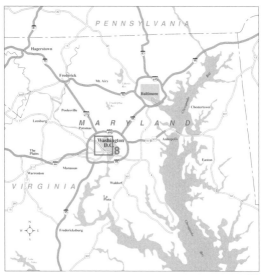

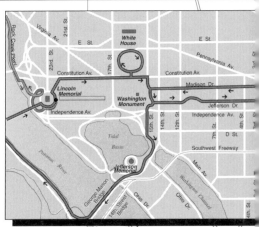

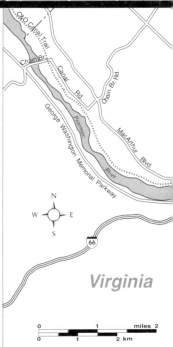

Note:

See page 164 for a map showing the locations of sights and places of interest in the Mall area.

Refer to page 166 for details on using bike paths to cross Arlington Memorial Bridge and George Mason Bridge.

Virginia

| 0 | | 1 | | miles 2 |
| 0 | 1 | | 2 km | |

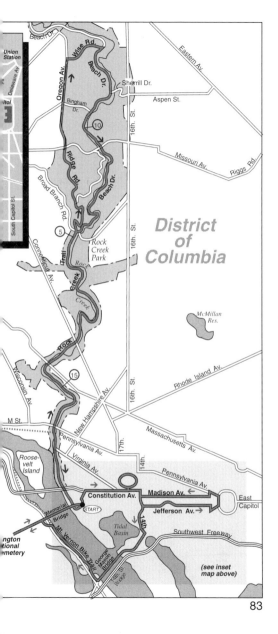

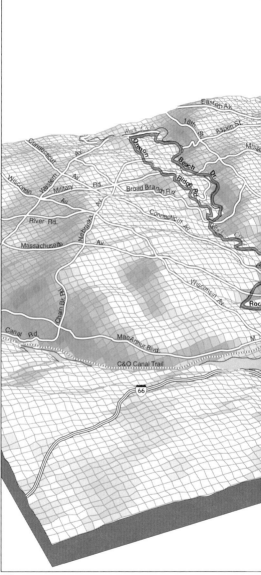

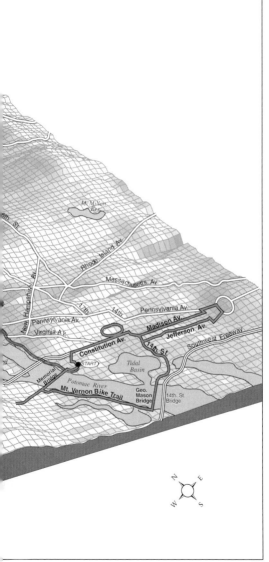

Rock Creek Park
17.4 miles

0   Begin in front of the Lincoln Memorial; get on the sidewalk as it comes off the south side of Memorial Bridge.
Loop under the bridge, following path as it heads back toward the Memorial.
Turn right on sidewalk at Parkway Dr.
Turn left at next intersection, cross the Parkway and get on the Rock Creek bike path.
Follow the off-road path through the Park to Broad Branch Rd.

5.1   Cross Broad Branch Rd. and head north on Ridge Rd.

5.8   Intersection with Ross Dr.

6.2   Bear right to stay on Ridge Rd.

6.6   Cross Military Rd. and join off-road bike path on right (east) side of Oregon Ave.

7.2   Intersection with Bingham Dr.

7.8   Turn right on Wise Rd.

8.4   Turn right on Beach Dr.

9.6   Intersection with Bingham Dr.; **join off-road bike path on west side of Beach Dr.**

10.1 Join Beach Dr. at Military Rd.

12.0 Join off-road bike path at Broad Branch Rd.

Retrace your route south on Rock Cr. bike path.

17.4 End at the Lincoln Memorial.

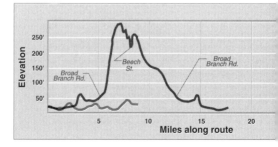

Monuments

8.4 miles

Begin at the Lincoln Memorial; head Northeast on Henry Bacon Dr.
- Turn right on Constitution Ave.
- Turn left on 16th St.; follow one-way road to the left around elipse in front of the White House.
- Turn left on 16th, then immediate left on Constitution Ave.
- Turn right on 15th St.
- Turn left on Jefferson Dr. (just past Washington Monument).
- Turn right on SW 3rd St., then immediate left on SW Maryland Ave.
- Turn left at circle in front of the Capitol.
- Turn left at circle onto Pennsylvania Ave.
- Turn left on NW 3rd St., then right on NW Madison Dr.
- Turn left on 15th St.
- Bear left onto Water St., then right on the road before 14th St. heading towards the Jefferson Memorial.
- Cross the George Mason Bridge on the right side.
- Exit the bridge onto Mt. Vernon Bike Trail and head north along the Potomac River to cross Memorial Parkway.
- Turn left onto bike path along Memorial Dr. toward Arlington National Cemetery.
- Entrance to Arlington National Cemetery; turn around and head east on Memorial Dr., to cross Memorial Bridge.
- End at the Lincoln Memorial.

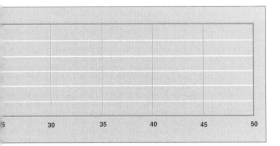

Notes:

Calorie Counter

Rock Creek Park: 17.4 miles

Average Speed (mph)	Riding Time	Calories Expended*
5	3 hrs. 29 mins.	480
10	1 hr. 44 mins.	510
15	1 hr. 10 mins.	630
20	52 mins.	920

Monuments: 8.4 miles

Average Speed (mph)	Riding Time	Calories Expended*
5	1 hr. 41 mins.	160
10	50 mins.	250
15	34 mins.	300
20	25 mins.	430

* Estimations from tractive-resistance calculations
Whitt and Wilson, "Bicycling Science"

Mount Vernon
Mt. Vernon Bike Trail
and
Alexandria

These two routes are almost entirely off-road. The Mt. Vernon Trail is one of the area's most popular routes, especially between Washington and Alexandria, for cyclists, joggers and walkers. South of Alexandria you'll encounter mostly cyclists, and can probably pick up your pace a little. The route through Alexandria and Arlington picks up a few streets along the way, but also incorporates part of Arlington's extensive off-road bike path system. Old Town Alexandria is a great place to find a meal or a treat, and there are plenty of places to picnic along the Mt. Vernon Trail.

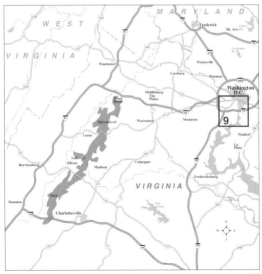

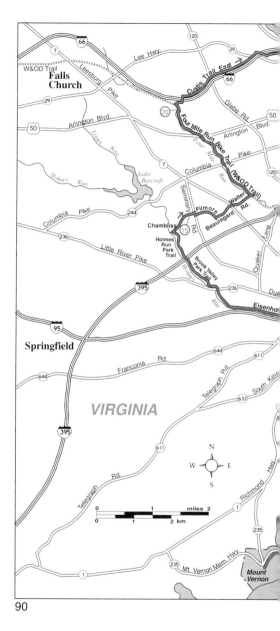

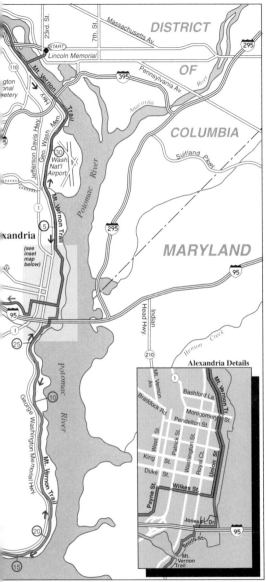

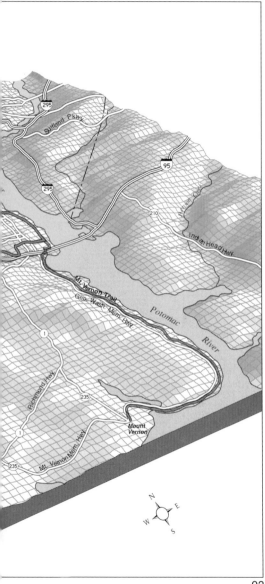

Mt. Vernon Bike Trail

33.8 miles

0   Begin at the Lincoln Memorial; head west across the Memorial Bridge on the south side.

0.7   Turn left at the end of the bridge onto bikepath that crosses the Geo. Wash. Memorial Pkwy.; head south on the Mt. Vernon Bike Trail along the Potomac River.

1.9   Cross under the 14th St. Bridge.

3.6   National Airport Metro Station.

5.6   Bear left where the path splits as you enter Alexandria.

6.8   Join Union Ave.

7.2   Old Town Alexandria. Follow the Mt. Vernon Trail signs at the south end of Alexandria to cross I-95 and then join the off-road bike path. Stay on the bike path all the way to Mt. Vernon.

16.9   Mt. Vernon.
      Note: Return to the Lincoln Memorial by the same route.

33.8   End at the Lincoln Memorial.

Alexandria (continued)

16.5   Intersection with Arlington Mill Dr.; **turn left onto bike path to join Four Mile Run Bike Trail (W & OD Trail).**

20.2   Turn right onto Custis Trail East at W & OD milepost 4; cross under I-66.

21.4   Intersection with Washington Blvd.

22.8   Intersection with Lee Hwy. (Hwy. 29).

24.6   Cross the Theodore Roosevelt bicycle bridge; head south on the Mt. Vernon Bike Trail.

25.7   Cross under the Arlington Memorial Bridge.

25.9   Turn right onto bike path to cross the Geo. Wash. Memorial Parkway.

26.1   Turn right to cross over Memorial Bridge.

26.8   End at the Lincoln Memorial.

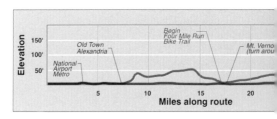

Alexandria

26.8 miles

Begin at the Lincoln Memorial; head west across the Memorial Bridge on the south side.

.7	**Turn left at the end of the bridge onto bikepath that crosses the Geo. Wash. Memorial Pkwy.;** head south on the Mt. Vernon Bike Trail along the Potomac River.
.9	Cross under the 14th St. Bridge.
.6	National Airport Metro Station.
.6	**Bear left where the path splits as you enter Alexandria.**
.8	Join Union Ave.
.2	Old Town Alexandria. Follow the Mt. Vernon Trail signs at the south end of Alexandria to cross I-95 and then join the off-road bike path. Stay on the bike path all the way to Mt. Vernon.
.4	**Turn right on bike path that enters a park and goes through a tunnel and joins Wilkes St.**
.8	Intersection with S. Washington St.
.1	**Turn left on Payne St.**
.6	Join bike path at the end of Payne St.
.1	Join Eisenhower Ave.
.6	Eisenhower Ave. Metro Station.
1.4	**Turn right onto bike path just before Eisenhower Ave. crosses a bridge;** follow bike path along Holmes Run.
3.3	Cross under I-395.
4.1	**Turn right onto bike path at Chambliss St.**
4.5	Join Chambliss St.
4.7	**Bear right onto Filmore Ave.**
5.2	**Turn right on Seminary, then immediate left on Filmore Ave.**
5.4	**Turn left on North Beauregard St.**
5.6	Intersection with Braddock Rd.; join bike path on left side of road.

(continued on left)

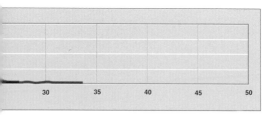

Notes:

_____

_____

_____

_____

_____

_____

_____

_____

_____

_____

_____

_____

_____

_____

_____

_____

_____

_____

Calorie Counter

Mt. Vernon Bike Trail: 33.8 miles

Average Speed (mph)	Riding Time	Calories Expended*
5	6 hrs. 46 mins.	920
10	3 hrs. 23 mins.	1030
15	2 hrs. 15 mins.	1290
20	1 hr. 41 mins.	1780

Alexandria: 26.8 miles

Average Speed (mph)	Riding Time	Calories Expended*
5	5 hrs. 22 mins.	730
10	2 hrs. 41 mins.	800
15	1 hr. 47 mins.	950
20	1 hr. 20 mins.	1390

* Estimations from tractive-resistance calculations
Whitt and Wilson, "Bicycling Science"

Purcellville
Short Hill Mtn.
and
Whites Ferry

There is plenty of great cycling in the area covered by these two routes. Many of the roads that lace the horse country of Loudoun County are lightly trafficked, two lane country roads — and these rides include some of the best. The Whites Ferry loop uses both the C&O Canal and the W&OD bike trails to good advantage, making a significant portion of a long ride on flat terrain. The W&OD Trail provides excellent cycling access to the area from Washington D.C., and Leesburg and Purcellville offer the accommodations, restaurants, and atmosphere to serve as a base for at least a weekend's worth of riding.

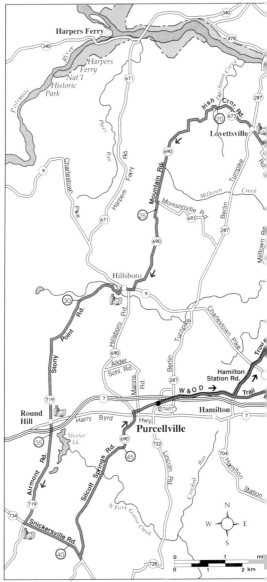

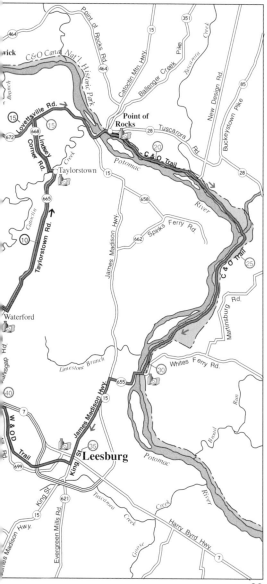

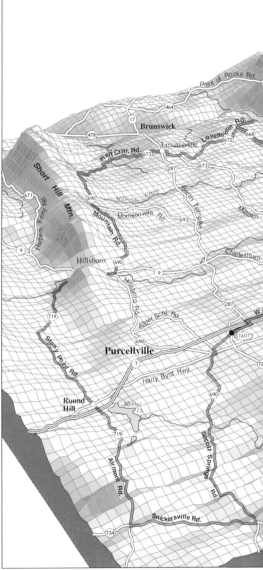

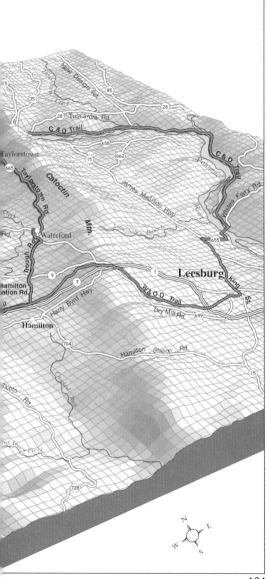

Short Hill Mtn.

47.7 miles

0	Begin at the Loudoun Valley High School on Maple Ave. in Purcellville; head north on Maple Ave.; **immediate right on the W & OD Regional Trail.**
3.0	**Turn left on Hamilton Station Rd. (Rt 704).**
4.3	Intersection with Charlestown Pike (Rt. 9).
6.4	**Turn left on Rt. 662.**
6.7	**Turn left to stay on Rt. 662.**
6.8	**Bear right onto Second St.**
7.1	**Turn right on Rt. 698.**
7.3	Continue straight onto Rt. 665/698.
7.4	Intersection where 698 turns right.
9.1	Intersection with Stumptown Rd. (Rt. 662).
10.7	Intersection with Bald Hill Rd.
12.7	**Turn left on Rt. 663; becomes Rt. 668.**
13.7	Intersection with Tankerfield Rd. (Rt. 669).
14.8	**Turn left on Lovettsville Rd. (Rt. 672);** becomes Broadway St. in Lovettsville.
18.4	Intersection with Berlin Turnpike (Rt. 287).
19.7	Intersection with Rt. 674.
20.2	Intersection with Georges Mill Rd. (Rt. 852).
20.9	Continue straight onto Irish Mtn. Rd. (Rt. 611) where Rt. 673 turns left; becomes Rt. 690.
23.8	Intersection with Britain Rd. (Rt. 682).
24.8	**Turn right to stay on Mountain Rd. (Rt. 690) where Morrisonville Rd. (Rt 693) continues straight.**
28.0	**Turn right on Charlestown Pike (Rt. 9).**
28.2	Intersection with Hillsboro Rd. (Rt 690).
28.6	**Turn left on Rt 719.**
30.0	**Turn left to stay on Rt. 719.**
30.7	Intersection with Short Hill Rd. (Rt 716).
33.0	Intersection with Alder School Rd. (Rt. 711).

(continued on page 104)

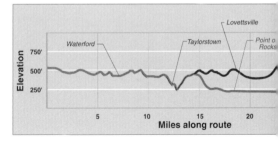

Whites Ferry

44.8 miles

●   Begin at the Loudoun Valley High School on Maple Ave. in Purcellville; head north on Maple Ave.; **immediate right on the W & OD Regional Trail.**

3.0   **Turn left on Hamilton Station Rd. (Rt 704).**

4.3   Intersection with Charlestown Pike (Rt. 9).

5.4   **Turn left on Rt. 662.**

5.7   **Turn left to stay on Rt. 662.**

5.8   **Bear right onto Second St.**

7.1   **Turn right on Rt. 698.**

7.3   Continue straight onto Rt. 665/698.

7.4   Intersection where 698 turns right.

9.1   Intersection with Stumptown Rd. (Rt. 662).

10.7   Intersection with Bald Hill Rd.

12.7   **Turn left on Rt. 663; becomes Rt. 668.**

13.7   Intersection with Tankerfield Rd. (Rt. 669).

14.8   **Turn right on Lovettsville Rd. (Rt. 672)** (caution - traffic).

17.5   **Turn left on Hwy. 15; cross over the Potomac River.**

17.9   **Bear right onto Rt 28; then immediate right on Commerce St.**

18.1   Enter C & O Canal National Historic Park - Point of Rocks; **turn left onto bike path just after crossing wooden bridge over Canal.**

21.7   Nolands Ferry boat landing.

24.2   Monocacy Aqueduct.

30.6   Whites Ferry; turn right on Whites Ferry Rd. (picnic area).

30.7   Cross Potomac River by ferry; ($.50 passengers, $2.25 vehicles) head west on Rt. 655.

32.1   **Turn left on James Madison Hwy. (Hwy 15).**

(continued on page 104)

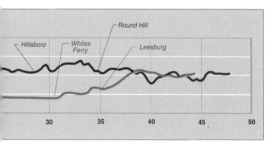

Short Hill Mtn. *(continued from page 102)*
34.8 Intersection with London St. (Rt. 7).
36.9 Intersection with Rt. 725.
38.3 Turn left on Snickersville Rd. (Rt. 734).
39.1 Intersection with Rt. 735.
40.8 Turn left on Silcott Springs Rd. (Rt. 690).
42.6 Intersection with Shoemaker School Rd.
(Rt. 622).
43.4 Intersection with Rt. 725.
45.9 Turn right on S. Nursery Ave.
46.6 Turn left on Rt. 7 then immediate right
on 21st St.
46.8 Turn right on W&OD Regional Trail.
47.7 End at the Loudoun Valley High School.

Whites Ferry (continued from page 103)
33.3 Continue straight onto Hwy. 15 Business.
35.1 Intersection with Market St. (Rt. 7).
35.4 Turn right on W&OD Regional Trail.
39.4 Cross over Rt. 7.
41.8 Intersection with Hamilton Station Rd.
(Rt. 704).
44.8 Turn left on Maple Ave.; end at Loudoun
Valley High School.

Calorie Counter

Short Hill Mtn.: 47.7 miles

Average Speed (mph)	Riding Time	Calories Expended*
5	9 hrs. 32 mins.	1310
10	4 hrs. 46 mins.	1430
15	3 hrs. 11 mins.	1830
20	2 hrs. 23 mins.	2510

Whites Ferry: 44.8 miles

Average Speed (mph)	Riding Time	Calories Expended*
5	8 hrs. 58 mins.	1230
10	4 hrs. 29 mins.	1350
15	2 hrs. 59 mins.	1710
20	2 hrs. 14 mins.	2350

* Estimations from tractive-resistance calculations
Whitt and Wilson, "Bicycling Science"

Middleburg
Blue Ridge
and
Horse Country

Country riding in the Washington area doesn't get much better than this! These two routes traverse the very beautiful horse country of Fauquier and Loudoun Counties, and provide the opportunity to venture into the Blue Ridge Mountains. The Blue Ridge route includes a challenging 2 mile ascent onto the ridge, and an occasional long distance view once you've made it. Be prepared for a fairly long and hilly ride when you tackle this one — and for a sense of accomplishment when you've finished it. The Horse Country loop is not quite as long, and covers mile after mile of very picturesque landscape.

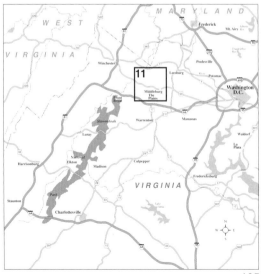

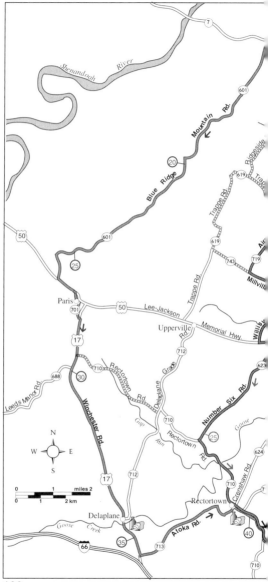

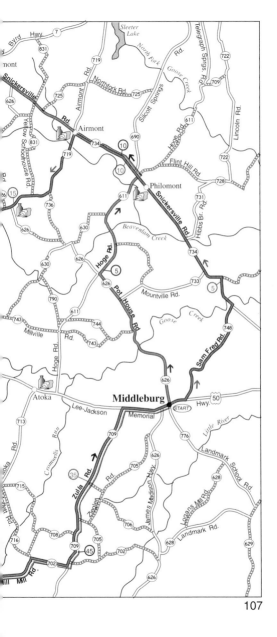

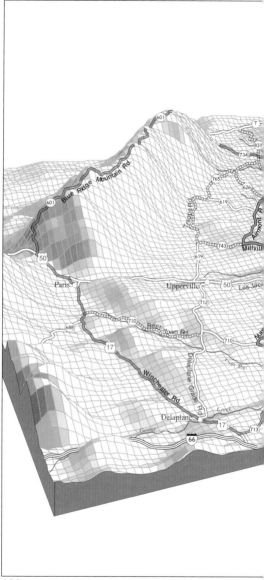

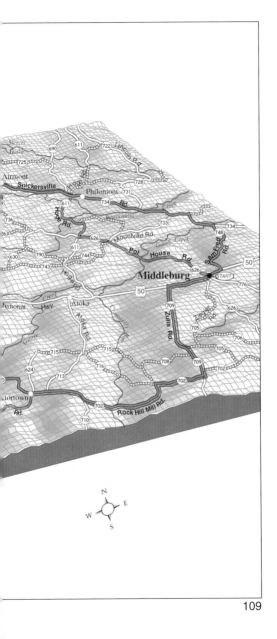

Blue Ridge

50.5 miles

0	Begin at intersection of Washington St. and Madison St. in Middleburg; head north on Madison St. (Rt. 626).
0.1	Middleburg School.
1.1	Intersection with Polecat Hill Rd. (Rt. 696).
2.6	Intersection with Rt. 744.
3.9	Intersection with Five Oaks Rd. (Rt. 745).
4.9	**Turn right on Hoge Rd. (Rt. 611).**
7.2	Intersection with Rt. 630.
8.6	**Turn left on Snickersville Rd. (Rt. 734).**
10.2	Intersection with Black Oak Rd. (Rt. 735).
10.9	Intersection with Airmont Rd. (Rt. 719).
12.3	Intersection with Yellow Schoolhouse Rd. (Rt. 831).
14.9	**Turn left on Harry Byrd Hwy. (Rt. 7)** (caution - traffic).
15.4	**Turn left on Blue Ridge Mtn. Rd. (Rt. 601).**
18.3	Intersection with Rt. 650.
26.7	**Turn left on Hwy. 50.** (caution - traffic).
27.4	**Bear left on Main St.**
27.7	**Bear right at Ashby Inn (Rt. 701).**
28.4	**Turn right on Rt. 17** (caution - heavy truck and auto traffic).
29.2	Entrance to Sky Meadows State Park.
29.4	Intersection with Rt. 710.
29.8	Intersection with Leeds Manor Rd. (Rt. 688).
32.8	Intersection with Pleasant Vale Rd. (Rt. 724).
34.0	Intersection with Rt. 623.
34.5	Intersection with Rt. 712.
35.1	Intersection with Rt. 55 W.
35.7	**Turn left on Atoka Rd. (Rt. 713).**
38.8	Intersection with Rt. 624.

(continued on page 112)

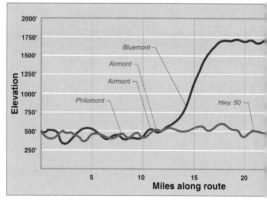

Horse Country

38.9 miles

Begin at intersection of Washington St. and Madison St. in Middleburg; head east on Washington St. (Hwy. 50).

.6 **Turn left on Sam Fred Rd. (Rt. 748).**
.1 **Turn left on Snickersville Rd. (Rt. 734).**
.1 Intersection with Lime Kiln Rd (Rt. 733).
.7 Intersection with Hibbs Bridge Rd. (Rt. 731).
.3 Intersection with Rt. 611 and Rt. 690.
1.0 Intersection with Black Oak Rd. (Rt. 735).
1.7 Turn left on Airmont Rd. (Rt. 719).
3.9 Intersection with Rt. 736.
5.1 Intersection with Rt. 626.
6.0 Intersection with Trappe Rd.
8.3 Turn left on Millville Rd. (Rt. 743).
9.7 Bear right onto Rt. 623.
1.3 Turn left on John Mosby Hwy. (Hwy. 50).
1.6 Turn right on Number Six Rd. (Rt. 623).
5.3 Turn left on Rt. 710 (unmarked).
7.7 Intersection with Rt. 713.
9.1 Turn left on Rt. 702.
0.6 Intersection with Rt. 762.
2.6 Turn left on Rt. 709.
7.6 Turn right on Hwy. 50; becomes Washington St.
8.9 End at intersection of Washington St. and Madison St. in Middleburg.

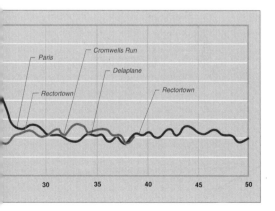

Blue Ridge (continued from page 110)

39.3 Turn right on Rectortown Rd. (Rt. 710).
39.7 Intersection with Rt. 713.
40.7 Turn left on Rt. 702.
42.2 Intersection with Rt. 762.
44.2 Turn left on Rt. 709.
49.2 Turn right on Hwy. 50; becomes
Washington St.
50.5 End at intersection of Washington St.
and Madison St. in Middleburg.

Notes:

Calorie Counter

Blue Ridge: 50.5 miles

Average Speed (mph)	Riding Time	Calories Expended*
5	10 hrs. 06 mins.	1380
10	5 hrs. 03 mins.	1520
15	3 hrs. 22 mins.	1940
20	2 hrs. 31 mins.	2610

Horse Country: 38.9 miles

Average Speed (mph)	Riding Time	Calories Expended*
5	7 hrs. 47 mins.	1100
10	3 hrs. 53 mins.	1220
15	2 hrs. 36 mins.	1550
20	1 hr. 57 mins.	2130

* Estimations from tractive-resistance calculations
Whitt and Wilson, "Bicycling Science"

The Plains
Warrenton
and
Bull Run Mtn.

These two rides meander through the rolling to hilly landscape of Fauquier and Loudoun Counties, and into the hearts of several of the area's historic towns. The roads are generally narrow, winding, and carry little traffic. One major exception is the stretch of Hwy. 17 between Warrenton and Rt. 628 - use extra caution on this 2.7 mile stretch. You'll find good views of the Blue Ridge Mountains and Bull Run Mtn. from many places along both routes, and a constantly changing landscape that includes open farmland, tree-lined roads, upscale horse farms and distant forests.

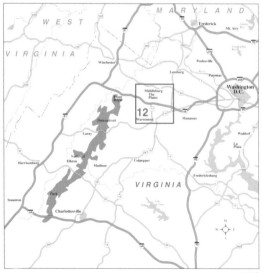

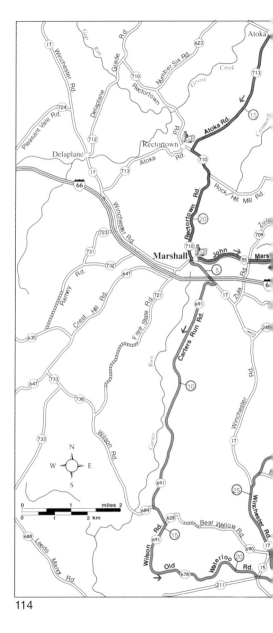

114

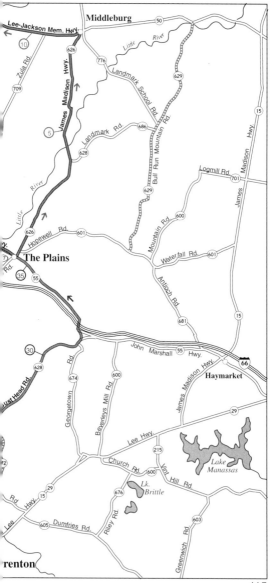

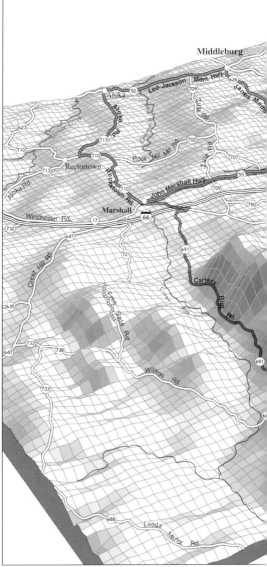

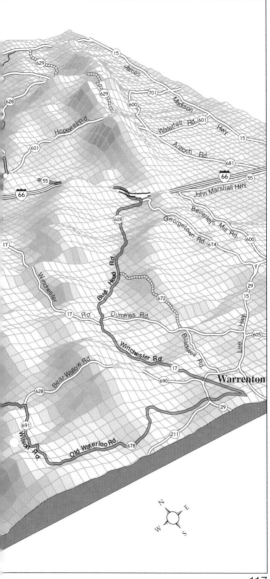

Warrenton

35.9 miles

0	Begin at the post office in The Plains on Rt. 245; head north on Rt. 245.
0.1	**Turn left on Main St. (Rt. 55);** becomes John Marshall Hwy.
1.1	Intersection with Rt. 704.
2.6	Intersection with Rt. 709.
3.3	Intersection with Rt. 622.
4.6	**Turn left on Warrenton Rd. (Business Rt. 17).**
5.4	Cross over I-66.
5.7	**Turn right on Carters Run Rd. (Rt. 691).**
14.2	**Turn left on Wilson Rd. to stay on Rt. 691.**
14.9	Intersection with Rt. 628.
16.7	Continue straight onto Rt. 678 where Rt. 691 turns right.
20.6	**Turn right on Rappahannock St. (unmarked); then left on Hwy. 211.**
20.7	Intersection with W. Shirley Ave. (Hwy's 17 & 29); becomes Waterloo St.
21.5	**Turn left on Hwy. 15 (Blackwell Rd.) then immediate left again onto Winchester St.**
22.8	Intersection with Hwy. 29 & 17; continue staight onto Hwy. 17 North (caution - narrow road with heavy traffic).
24.7	Intersection with Rt. 628.
25.5	**Turn right on Rt. 628/Rt. 605.**
25.7	Intersection with Rt. 605.
27.5	Intersection with Rt. 672.
28.6	Intersection with Rt. 694.
31.8	Intersection with Rt. 674.
32.0	Continue straight onto Rt. 674.
32.3	**Turn left on John Marshall Hwy. (Rt. 55).**
34.4	Intersection with Rt. 698.
35.8	**Turn left on Fauquier Ave. (Rt. 245).**
35.9	End at the post office.

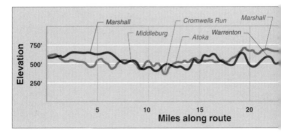

Bull Run Mtn.

26.3 miles

Begin at the post office in The Plains on Rt. 245; head north on Rt. 245.

1	**Turn right on Main St. (Rt. 55).**
2	**Turn left on Rt. 626.**
3	Intersection with Rt. 601.
6	Intersection with Rt. 705.
5	Intersection with Rt. 702.
0	Intersection with Rt. 679.
7	Intersection with Rt. 706.
6	Winery.
6	Intersection with Rt. 627.
5	Intersection with Rt. 807.
4	**Turn left on Washington St.;** becomes Hwy. 50.
6	Intersection with Rt. 709.
0.3	Intersection with Rt. 754.
1.7	Intersection with Rt. 611.
2.3	**Turn left on Atoka Rd. (Rt 713); then left again to stay on Rt. 713.**
3.8	Intersection with Rt. 714.
5.4	Intersection with Rt. 715/716.
7.5	**Turn left on Rectortown Rd. (Rt. 710).**
3.5	Intersection with Rt. 702.
1.6	**Turn left on Main St.;** becomes Rt. 55.
3.6	Intersection with Rt. 709.
5.1	Intersection with Rt. 704.
6.2	**Turn right on Rt. 245.**
6.3	End at the post office in The Plains.

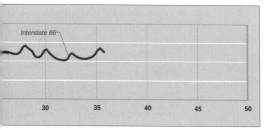

Notes:

Calorie Counter

Warrenton: 35.9 miles

Average Speed (mph)	Riding Time	Calories Expended*
5	7 hrs. 11 mins.	1020
10	3 hrs. 35 mins.	1130
15	2 hrs. 24 mins.	1430
20	1 hr. 48 mins.	1960

Bull Run Mtn.: 26.3 miles

Average Speed (mph)	Riding Time	Calories Expended*
5	5 hrs. 16 mins.	720
10	2 hrs. 38 mins.	790
15	1 hr. 45 mins.	940
20	1 hr. 19 mins.	1370

* Estimations from tractive-resistance calculations
Whitt and Wilson, "Bicycling Science"

Haymarket
Cedar Run
and
Manassas

These two rides incorporate a wide variety of riding conditions and landscapes — from two lane country roads through open and rolling farmlands to the intensity of urban Manassas. There is plenty of good country cycling to be found in the area, though, and in general you'll discover it further away from Manassas. Use extra caution when entering the city from the south and leaving from the north, where you will be cycling through an area of heavy commercial activity. The National Battlefield Park has picnic areas, hiking trails, a Visitor Center, and, of course, great historic interest.

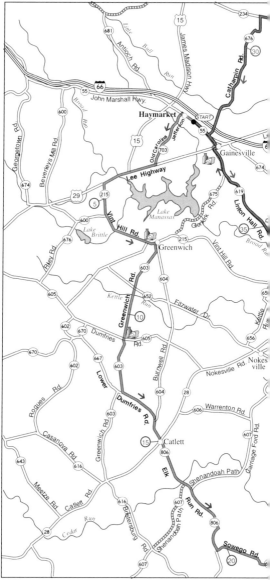

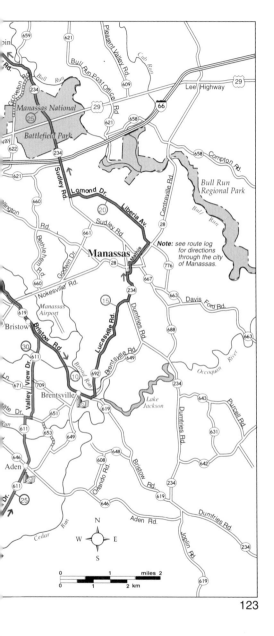

Note: see route log for directions through the city of Manassas.

Cedar Run

39.7 miles

0	Begin at the Gainesville Elementary School on Rt. 55 in Haymarket; head northwest on Rt. 55.
0.4	**Turn left on Jefferson St. (Rt. 625).**
0.9	Continue straight onto Old Carolina Rd. (Rt. 703) where Rt. 625 bears off to right.
1.3	Intersection with Carver Rd. (Rt. 647).
2.5	**Turn right on Lee Hwy. (Rt. 29)** (caution - traffic).
3.4	Intersection with Hwy. 15.
4.4	**Turn left on Vint Hill Rd. (Rt. 215).**
7.5	**Turn right on Greenwich Rd. (Rt. 603).**
9.2	Intersection with Rt. 652.
10.4	Intersection with Rt. 669.
11.0	Intersection with Dumphries Rd. (Rt. 605).
12.8	Intersection with Rt. 667; becomes Rt. 667.
14.3	Intersection with Rt. 604.
15.0	Intersection with Catlett Rd. (Rt. 28); becomes Rt. 806.
16.9	Intersection with Rt. 607.
19.5	**Turn left on Sowego Rd. (Rt. 611).**
21.2	**Turn left to stay on Rt. 611 at intersection with Rt. 612.**
22.9	**Turn left to stay on Rt. 611.**
23.3	One lane bridge over Cedar Run.
24.8	Intersection with Hazelwood Dr. (Rt. 645).
26.3	Intersection with Aden Rd. (Rt. 646).
28.0	**Turn right on Parkgate Dr. (Rt. 653).**
28.2	**Turn left on Valley View Dr. (Rt. 611).**
29.2	Intersection with Colvin Lane (Rt. 671).
30.9	**Turn left on Bristow Rd. (Rt. 619).**
32.4	Intersection with Nokesville Rd. (Rt. 28).
34.6	Intersection with Devlin Rd. (Rt. 621).
38.4	**Turn right on Lee Hwy. (Hwy. 29); then immediate left on Gallerher Rd.**
38.7	Straight onto John Marshall Hwy. (Rt. 55).
39.7	End at Gainesville Elementary School.

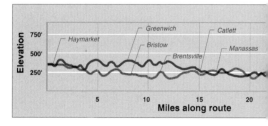

Manassas

34.7 miles

)	Begin at the Gainesville Elementary School on Rt. 55 in Haymarket; head southeast on Rt. 55.
1.0	Continue straight onto Gallerher Rd.
1.3	**Turn right on Rt. 29, then immediate left on Linton Hall Rd. (Rt. 619).**
2.3	Intersection with Glenkirk Rd. (Rt. 675).
7.3	Intersection with Nokesville Rd. (Rt. 28).
8.8	Intersection with Valley View Rd. (Rt. 611).
10.8	Intersection with Hooe Rd. (Rt. 651).
11.3	Intersection with Old Church Rd. (Rt. 649).
11.5	Brentsville Park, picnic area.
11.8	**Turn left on Lucasville Rd. (Rt. 692);** continue straight where Rt. 649 turns right.
12.1	Bridge over Broad Run.
14.3	Intersection with Goodwin Dr. (Rt. 661).
15.2	**Turn right on Hastings Dr.**
15.6	**Turn left on Dumfries Rd. (Rt. 234).**
16.1	Continue straight where Richmond Ave. turns right; becomes Grant Ave.
16.7	**Turn right on Prince William St.**
16.9	**Turn left on Main St.**
17.2	**Turn right on Mathis Ave.**
17.5	Intersection with Sudley Rd. (Rt. 234).
18.1	**Turn left on Liberia Ave.**
18.8	Intersection with Kirby St.
19.2	Intersection with Stonewall Rd.
19.6	Becomes Lomond S. Rd.
20.0	Becomes Lomond Dr.
20.5	Intersection with Damascus Dr.
21.6	**Turn right on Sudley Rd. (Rt. 234)** (caution - traffic and congestion).
22.9	Cross under I-66.
23.7	Entrance to Manassas National Battlefield Park Visitors Center.
24.2	Intersection with Lee Hwy. (Rt. 29).
24.7	Dogan Ridge picnic area.

(continued on page 128)

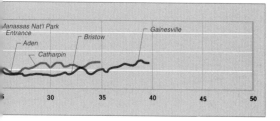

26.5 Intersection with Rt. 659.
28.1 Intersection with Pageland Lane (Rt. 705).
29.1 Turn left on Catharpin Rd. (Rt. 676).
30.9 Intersection with Artemus Rd. (Rt. 704).
33.6 Cross over I-66.
33.9 Turn right on John Marshall Hwy. (Rt. 55).
34.7 End at the Gainesville Elementary School.

Notes:

Calorie Counter

Cedar Run: 39.7 miles

Average Speed (mph)	Riding Time	Calories Expended*
5	7 hrs. 56 mins.	1090
10	3 hrs. 58 mins.	1200
15	2 hrs. 39 mins.	1520
20	1 hr. 59 mins.	2090

Manassas: 34.7 miles

Average Speed (mph)	Riding Time	Calories Expended*
5	6 hrs. 56 mins.	980
10	3 hrs. 28 mins.	1090
15	2 hrs. 19 mins.	1390
20	1 hr. 44 mins.	1900

* Estimations from tractive-resistance calculations
Whitt and Wilson, "Bicycling Science"

Culpeper
Rappahannock River
and
Battle Mtn.

These two routes cover an area ranging from the hilly base of the Blue Ridge Mountains to the gently rolling terrain of the Rappahannock and Rapidan River valleys. There is an interesting mixture of scenery along the routes, including farms and forests and the often-present view of the Blue Ridge Mtn. skyline. You'll find several places to rest and buy food, especially on the Battle Mtn. loop. Some of the roads may have a loose gravel cover over the asphalt, and you should ride these carefully — most noteably on corners and downhill stretches.

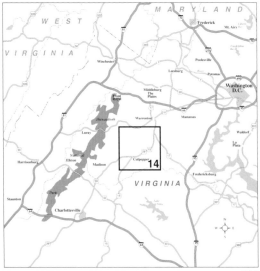

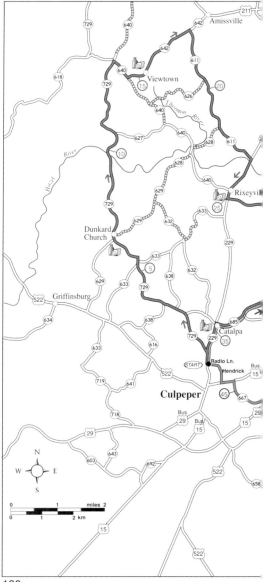

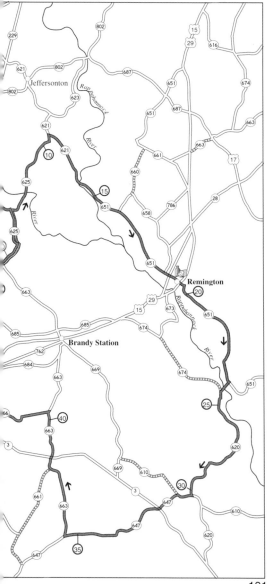

Jeffersonton

Remington

Brandy Station

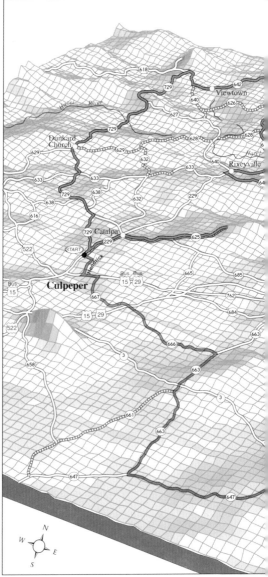

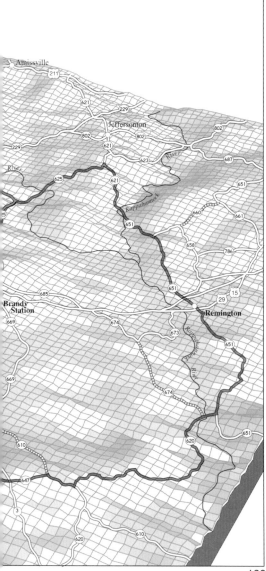

133

Rappahannock River

46.8 miles

0	Begin at the Binns Elementary School just north of Culpeper on Rt. 229; head north on Rt. 229.
0.5	Intersection with Rt. 729.
1.7	**Turn right on Rt. 685.**
3.0	**Turn left on Rt. 625.**
5.4	Intersection with Rt. 711.
6.0	Intersection with Rt. 663.
8.4	**Turn right to stay on Rt. 625.**
10.7	Intersection with Rt. 621.
11.7	**Turn right to stay on Rt. 621.**
13.9	Cross over Rappahannock River.
14.1	Continue straight onto Rt. 651.
16.9	Intersection with Rt. 659.
18.8	Intersection with Hwys. 15 & 29.
19.2	Intersection with James Madison St. in Remington.
19.4	Cross RR tracks; **bear right to stay on Rt. 651.**
22.0	Intersection with Rt. 668.
24.2	**Turn right on Rt. 620.**
24.6	Cross Rappahannock River.
24.7	**Turn left to stay on Rt. 620.**
27.3	Intersection with Rt. 682.
30.1	**Turn right on Rt. 610.**
30.7	**Bear left onto Rt. 647.**
31.6	**Turn right on Rt. 3; then immediate left on Rt. 647.**
33.8	Intersection with Rt. 680.
35.7	**Turn right on Rt. 663.**
38.4	Intersection with Rt. 661.
38.7	Intersection with Rt. 3.
40.4	**Turn left on Rt. 666.**
42.9	Intersection with Rt. 703.
43.5	**Cross Hwys. 29 & 15 then immediate left on Rt. 667.**
44.7	Intersection with Kaiser Rd. (Rt. 699).

(continued)

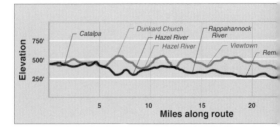

Battle Mtn.

36.5 miles

Begin at the Binns Elementary School just north of Culpeper on Rt. 229; head north on Rt. 229.

.5	**Turn left on Rt. 729.**
.1	Intersection with Rt. 685.
2.6	Intersection with Rt. 638 (north).
.1	Intersection with Rt. 638 (south).
.3	Intersection with Rt. 633.
.8	Intersection with Rt. 629.
.7	Intersection with Rt. 628.
.9	Cross Hazel River.
0.8	Intersection with Rt. 627.
2.4	Intersection with Rt. 676.
3.9	**Turn right on Rt. 640.**
4.6	**Bear left onto Rt. 642.**
5.4	Intersection with Rt. 646.
7.5	Intersection with Rt. 611 (north).
7.6	**Turn right on Rt. 611 (south).**
9.7	Intersection with Rt. 626.
1.5	Intersection with Rt. 628.
3.3	**Turn right on Rt. 229.**
4.8	Intersection with Rt. 640 (west).
5.1	**Turn left on Rt. 640. (east).**
6.4	Intersection with Rt. 630.
8.2	**Turn right on Rt. 625.**
0.6	Intersection with Rt. 663.
3.5	**Turn right on Rt. 685.**
4.8	**Turn left on Rt. 229.**
6.5	End at the Binns Elementary School.

Rappahannock River (continued)

5.5	**Turn left on James Madison Hwy. (Bus. 15).**
6.2	**Turn right on Hendrick St.**
6.6	**Bear left onto Radio Lane.**
6.8	End at Main St. and the Binns Elementary School.

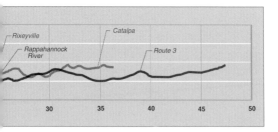

Calorie Counter

Rappahannock River: 46.8 miles

Average Speed (mph)	Riding Time	Calories Expended*
5	9 hrs. 22 mins.	1280
10	4 hrs. 41 mins.	1410
15	3 hrs. 07 mins.	1800
20	2 hrs. 20 mins.	2460

Battle Mtn.: 36.5 miles

Average Speed (mph)	Riding Time	Calories Expended*
5	7 hrs. 18 mins.	1030
10	3 hrs. 39 mins.	1150
15	2 hrs. 26 mins.	1460
20	1 hr. 49 mins.	1990

* Estimations from tractive-resistance calculations
Whitt and Wilson, "Bicycling Science"

Madison
Old Rag
and
Gordonsville

Although both of these routes are fairly long, there are several ways to shorten them and still experience the rural flavor of Madison County. For the most part the roads wind through a mixture of forest and farmland, carry little traffic, and offer some good views of the Blue Ridge Mountains. Watch for more traffic on those roads that link the larger towns, though, and be especially careful on the short segment of Hwy. 29. The ride between Madison and Old Rag is exceptionally pleasant — for its scenery and for its relative flatness — and would make a great out-and-back trip with a picnic stop at the base of Old Rag Mtn.

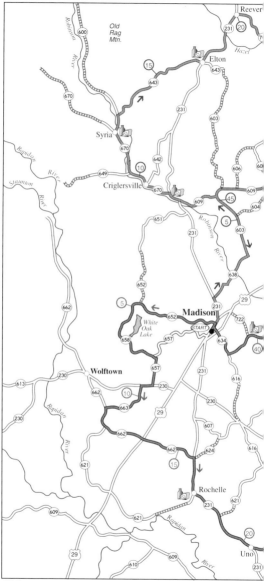

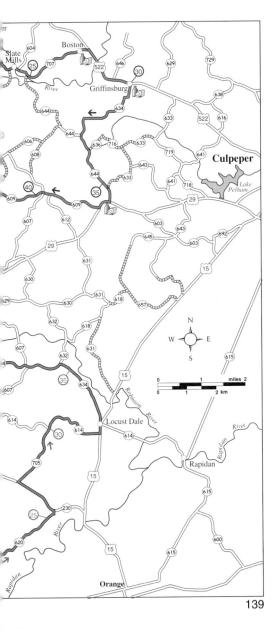

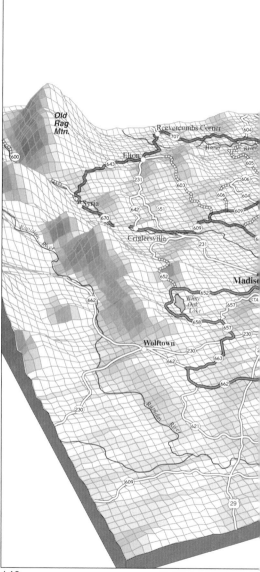

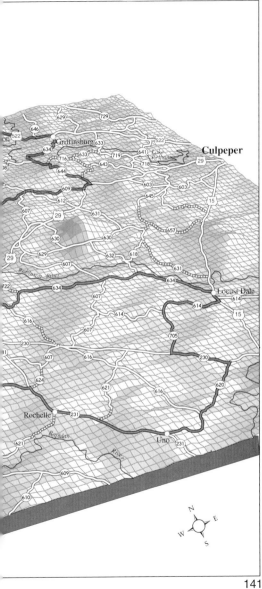

Old Rag

51.1 miles

0   Begin at the County Courthouse at Main St. and Church St. in Madison; head north on Main St.

0.4   **Bear left onto Rt. 231.**

1.3   **Turn right on Rt. 638.**

2.2   Intersection with Rt. 653.

3.5   **Turn left on Rt. 603.**

5.1   Intersection with Rt. 604.

6.2   **Turn left on Rt. 609.**

8.0   **Turn right on Rt. 231.**

8.6   **Turn left on Rt. 670.**

9.5   Intersection with Rt. 642.

10.4   Intersection with Rt. 649.

12.2   **Turn right on Rt. 643.**

13.0   **Turn right to stay on Rt. 643** (Rt. 600 continues straight to the base of Old Rag Mtn.).

14.1   Intersection with Rt. 720.

16.6   Intersection with Rt. 645.

17.4   **Turn left on Rt. 231.**

18.0   Intersection with Rt. 646.

19.1   Intersection with Rt. 602.

20.0   **Turn right on Rt. 707.**

23.1   Intersection with Rt. 607.

23.9   Intersection with Rt. 604.

24.8   Intersection with Rt. 644.

27.0   Intersection with Rt. 650.

27.4   **Turn right to stay on Rt. 707.**

27.7   **Turn right on Hwy. 522.**

29.4   Intersection with Rt. 646.

30.0   **Turn right on Rt. 634.**

32.8   **Turn left on Rt. 637.**

33.5   **Turn left on Rt. 644.**

35.2   Intersection with Rt. 715.

36.6   **Turn right on Hwy. 29**
(caution - traffic).

(continued on page 144)

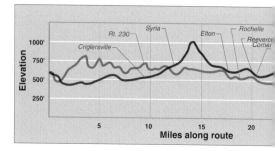

Gordonsville

43.1 miles

Begin at the County Courthouse at Main St. and Church St. in Madison; head north on Main St.

.3 **Turn left on Ruth Rd. (Rt. 652).**
.6 Continue straight onto Rt. 656.
.1 **Bear left onto Rt. 658.**
.8 Continue straight onto Rt. 657.
.0 **Turn right on Rt. 230.**
.3 **Turn left on Rt. 663.**
1.3 **Turn left on Rt. 662.**
2.1 Intersection with Rt. 621.
3.7 Intersection with Hwy. 29.
6.0 **Bear right onto Old Blue Ridge Parkway (Rt. 231).**
7.2 Intersection with Rt. 621.
8.7 Intersection with Rt. 621.
0.6 **Turn left on Rt. 620.**
2.0 **Turn left on Rt. 616.**
2.5 **Bear right onto Rt. 620.**
5.7 **Turn left on Rt. 230 (unmarked).**
7.1 **Turn right on Rt. 684.**
7.5 **Turn right on Rt. 705.**
8.2 Intersection with Rt. 622.
0.0 Continue straight onto Rt. 614.
2.5 **Turn left on Hwy. 15.**
3.0 **Turn left on Rt. 634.**
5.9 Intersection with Rt. 632.
7.2 Intersection with Rt. 607.
0.5 Intersection with Rt. 722.
1.6 **Turn right to stay on Rt. 634.**
2.7 Intersection with Hwy. 29.
3.0 **Turn left on Main St.**
3.1 End at the Courthouse in Madison.

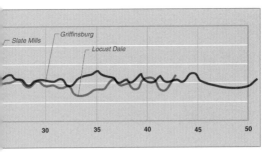

37.0 Turn right on Rt. 609.
39.2 Intersection with Rt. 640.
39.5 Intersection with Rt. 607.
41.8 Intersection with Rt. 605.
42.7 Intersection with Rt. 604.
44.6 Intersection with Rt. 603.
44.9 Turn left on Rt. 603.
47.6 Turn right on Rt. 638.
49.8 Turn left on Rt. 231.
50.7 Turn right on Main St.
51.1 End at the Courthouse in Madison.

Notes:

Calorie Counter

Old Rag: 51.1 miles

Average Speed (mph)	Riding Time	Calories Expended*
5	10 hrs. 13 mins.	1400
10	5 hrs. 06 mins.	1540
15	3 hrs. 24 mins.	1960
20	2 hrs. 33 mins.	2640

Gordonsville: 43.1 miles

Average Speed (mph)	Riding Time	Calories Expended*
5	8 hrs. 37 mins.	1180
10	4 hrs. 19 mins.	1300
15	2 hrs. 52 mins.	1650
20	2 hrs. 09 mins.	2260

* Estimations from tractive-resistance calculations
Whitt and Wilson, "Bicycling Science"

Shenandoah National Park

Skyline Drive

Shenandoah National Park is one of the most visited parks in the National Park System. On a clear day the views from the many pull-outs along Skyline Drive are stunning, and give you a real appreciation for the geography of the Appalachian region. While the climb up to the ridge is strenuous, the trip through the Park along the crest of the Appalachian Mountains is less demanding. There are many good places for picnicking and a few restaurants and food stores along the route. The Park Service accepts, but does not encourage, the use of Skyline Drive for cycling — especially during the fall foliage season. Be extra cautious on this ride.

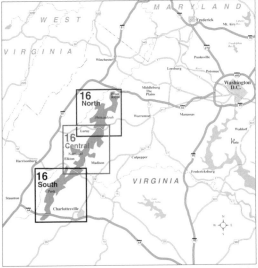

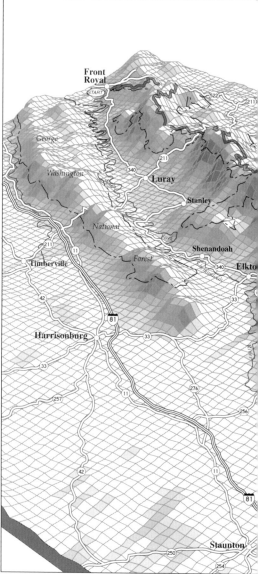

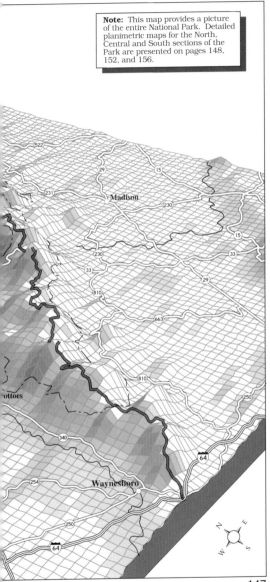

Note: This map provides a picture of the entire National Park. Detailed planimetric maps for the North, Central and South sections of the Park are presented on pages 148, 152, and 156.

Madison

Waynesboro

ottoes

Shenandoah National Park
North Section

Woodstock

George Washington National Forest

Rileyville

Springfield

Luray

Shenan

Mathew Campgr

Elkwallow Wayside

Jeremys Gap

Thor Holl

Bashm Gap

Skyline Drive

Pass Mtn.

Panorama

Skyline

Drive

North Fork Shenandoah River

South Fork Shenandoah River

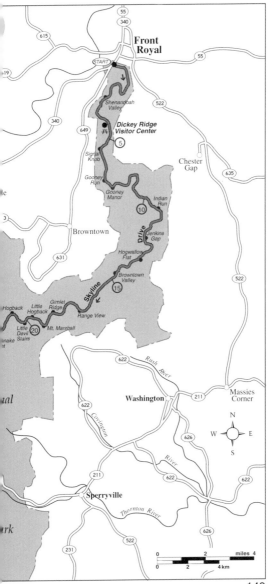

Shenandoah National Park

North Section

31.5 miles

0	Begin at the North gate entrance to park; entrance fee is $2.00 for cyclists.
2.8	Shenandoah Valley overlook.
4.6	**Dickey Ridge Visitor Center;** information, exhibits, toilets, water, picnic area, phone.
5.7	Signal Knob overlook.
6.8	Gooney Run overlook.
7.3	Gooney Manor overlook.
10.8	Indian Run overlook.
12.4	Jenkins Gap overlook.
13.8	Hogwallow Flats overlook.
14.9	Browntown Valley overlook; water.
17.1	Range View overlook.
18.4	Gimlet Ridge overlook.
19.0	Mt. Marshall overlook.
19.7	Little Hogback overlook.

(continued)

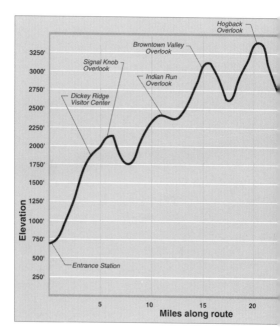

Directions from Front Royal to Park entrance

Begin at Visitors Centers/Chamber of Commerce at Main
St. & High St. in Front Royal; head west on Main St.
Turn left on Royal Ave.
Intersection with South St. (Rt. 55).
Turn left into Shenandoah NP.

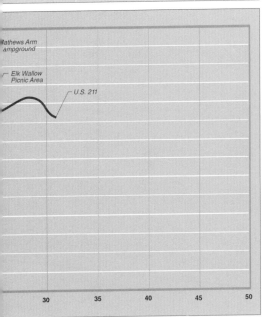

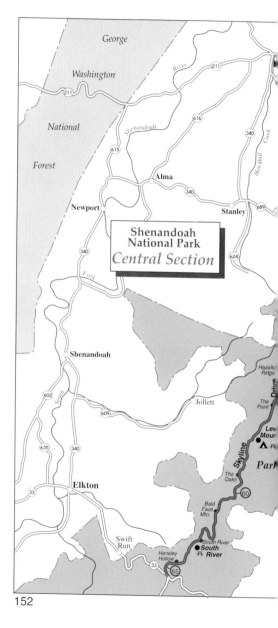

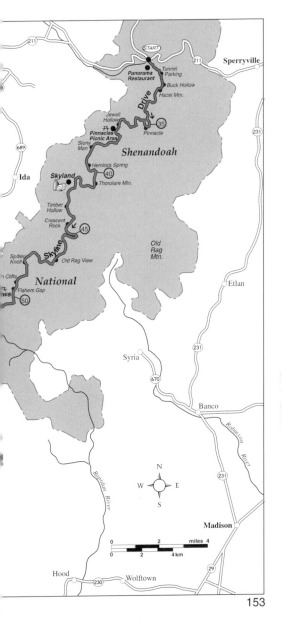

START

Tunnel Parking

Panorama Restaurant

Buck Hollow

Hazel Mtn.

Sperryville

211

Drive

35

Pinnacle

Jewell Hollow

Pinnacles Picnic Area

Stony Man

Shenandoah

689

Ida

Hemlock Spring

Skyland

40

Thorofare Mtn.

Timber Hollow

Crescent Rock

45

Skyline

Old Rag View

Spitler Knoll

n Cliffs

National

Fishers Gap

ws

50

Old Rag Mtn.

231

Etlan

Syria

670

Banco

Robinson River

Rapidan River

N

W E

S

Madison

0   2   miles 4

0   2   4 km

231

29

Hood

Wolftown

230

Shenandoah National Park

Central Section

33.9 miles

31.6 Panorama development; information, food, toilet, phone.
32.4 Tunnel Parking overlook.
33.0 Hazel Mtn. overlook; water.
35.1 Pinnacles overlook.
35.4 Jewel Hollow overlook; water.
36.7 Pinnacles Picnic Area; toilets, water, sheltered picnic tables.
38.6 Stony Man Mtn. overlook; water, toilets.
39.7 Hemlock Springs overlook; water.
40.5 Thorofare Mtn. overlook.
41.7 North entrance to Skyland; food, toilets, water, phone.
42.5 South entrance to Skyland.
43.3 Timber Hollow overlook.
44.4 Crescent Rock overlook.
46.5 Old Rag View overlook.
46.7 Upper Hawkskill Parking; water.
48.1 Spitler Knoll overlook.
49.0 Franklin Cliffs overlook.
49.4 Fishers Gap overlook.
51.0 North entrance to Big Meadows; visitor center.
51.2 South entrance to Big Meadows; food, picnic area, water, toilets, phone.

(continued)

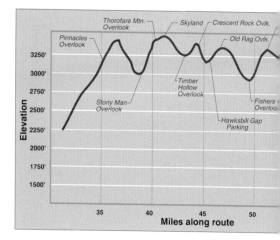

154

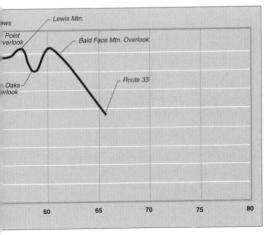

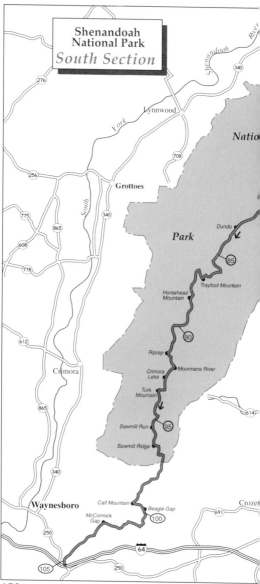

Shenandoah
National Park
South Section

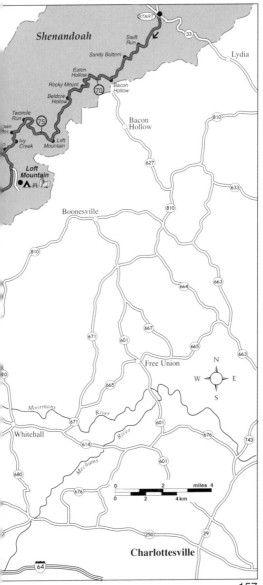

START

Shenandoah

Swift Run

Sandy Bottom

Eaton Hollow

Rocky Mount

70

Beldore Hollow

Bacon Hollow

Twomile Run

75

own tn

Ivy Creek

Loft Mountain

Loft Mountain ●▲ 🚻 📷

Bacon Hollow

Boonesville

Lydia

33

810

627

633

810

664

663

671

601

667

665

663

Free Union

N
W ● E
S

665

Moormans River

671

River

601

676

743

Whitehall

614

River

Mechums

601

680

676

0   2   miles 4

0   2   4 km

250

29

Charlottesville

64

Shenandoah National Park

South Section

39.9 miles

65.5 Intersection with Hwy. 33.
67.2 Swift Run overlook.
67.8 Sandy Bottom overlook.
69.3 Bacon Hollow overlook.
70.6 Eaton Hollow overlook.
71.2 Rocky Mount overlook.
72.2 Beldor Hollow overlook.
74.4 Loft Mtn. overlook.
76.2 Two Mile Run overlook.
76.9 Brown Mtn. overlook.
77.5 Ivy Creek overlook.
78.1 Rockytop overlook.
79.5 Loft Mtn. development; food, toilets, water
campground, picnic area, phone; open
May - October.
81.2 Big Run overlook.
81.9 Doyles River overlook.
83.7 Dundo overlook.
86.8 Trayfoot Mtn. overlook; water.
88.6 Horsehead overlook.
91.4 Riprap overlook.
92.0 Moormans River overlook.
92.6 Crimora Lake overlook.
93.7 Turk Mtn. overlook.
95.3 Sawmill Run overlook.
95.9 Sawmill Ridge overlook.
98.9 Calf Mtn. overlook.
99.8 Beagle Gap overlook.
102.4 McCormick Gap overlook.
105.4 Intersection with Hwy. 250 & I-64.

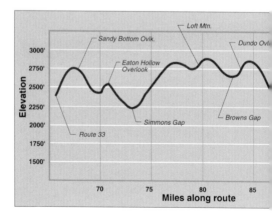

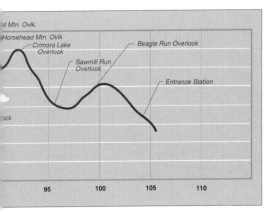

ot Mtn. Ovlk.

Horsehead Mtn. Ovlk.
Crimora Lake
Overlook

Beagle Run Overlook

Sawmill Run
Overlook

Entrance Station

ock

95	100	105	110

Calorie Counter

North Section: 31.5 miles

Average Speed (mph)	Riding Time	Calories Expended*
5	6 hrs. 18 mins.	870
10	3 hrs. 09 mins.	940
15	2 hrs. 06 mins.	1230
20	1 hr. 34 mins.	1650

Central Section 33.9 miles

Average Speed (mph)	Riding Time	Calories Expended*
5	6 hrs. 47 mins.	930
10	3 hrs. 23 mins.	1030
15	2 hrs. 16 mins.	1300
20	1 hr. 42 mins.	1790

South Section: 39.9 miles

Average Speed (mph)	Riding Time	Calories Expended*
5	8 hrs. 37 mins.	1090
10	4 hrs. 19 mins.	1200
15	2 hrs. 52 mins.	1530
20	2 hrs. 09 mins.	2100

* Estimations from tractive-resistance calculations
Whitt and Wilson, "Bicycling Science"

Around the D.C. Area

Major Off-Road Bike Trails

The routes outlined in this book give you a detailed look at some of the best on-road cycling in the Washington area. A few use portions of an extensive network of off-road bike trails to complete a loop, but don't cover this trail system fully. The following will help to fill in the details about the more popular of these bike trails. They are sometimes crowded on pleasant weekends, but always offer the chance to escape from the congestion of city streets and to enjoy more of the area's natural beauty. The trails often follow streams or lake shorelines and are often shaded and cool on hot days.

Rock Creek Park

This trail follows Rock Creek from the Potomac River in Georgetown to Lake Needwood in Rockville - a total of 23 miles. The lower section is covered by the Rock Creek Park route on Map 8. The upper section, from Lake Needwood to Grosvenor Lane, is included in the Lake Needwood route of Map 4. In between, the paved trail winds through trees and along the creek. There are no places to buy food in the Park until you reach Lake Needwood, so bring your lunch if you plan to picnic.

The Shady Grove Metro Station is not far from Lake Needwood, offering a quick return on a one-way ride (see page 163 for Metro information). To get there, turn left on Lake Needwood Rd. at the north end of the lake, then left again on Redland Rd.

Chesapeake & Ohio (C&O) Canal National Historic Park

This 184.5 mile hiker/biker path starts in Georgetown and ends in Cumberland, Maryland. It is a hard packed dirt trail that gets rougher both further north and after a heavy rainfall. In general it has a good surface for cycling, though the fat tires of an all-terrain bike might be the most comfortable.

If you are travelling any distance on the towpath, it is wise to carry the tools and materials recommended in the Cycling Information chapter. A rough and muddy section of trail can be hard on your bike — especially the chain, tires, spokes and gears. The National Park Service prints a map of the Park that shows parking lots and facilities along the entire length of the towpath.

Day trips on the lower section could include a picnic along the Potomac or a snack from the concessions at Fletcher's Boathouse (milepost 2.5), Great Falls Tavern (milepost 15), Swains Lock (milepost 17), or Seneca Creek (milepost 23).

Hiker/biker overnight campsites for tent camping occur about every five miles between Horsepen Branch (milepost 25) and Evitts Creek (milepost 180). Camping supplies, ice, food and beverages can be bought at stores on access roads that cross the Park.

There are two sections of the towpath to avoid. At milepost 12 (travelling north) follow Berma Rd. on the berm side of the Canal at Old Anglers Inn and return to the towpath at the stop lock above Lock 16 at milepost 13.6. Further up, between Dam 4 at milepost 84.5 and Lock 41 at milepost 88.9, the road detour shown below is recommended. There

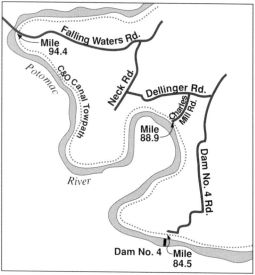

no canal in this stretch and the towpath is sometimes narrow, close to the river's edge and very rocky. Also, during periods of high river level use the alternate route shown on the map all the way to milepost 94.4.

Mount Vernon Trail
This trail is detailed on Map 9.

Washington and Old Dominion (W&OD) Railroad Regional Park
An old railroad right-of-way, converted to a park with a paved trail, constitutes the bulk of this Regional Park. Beginning in Arlington, at the intersection of Shirlington Dr. and Four Mile Run Dr., it runs 45 almost flat miles into the Virginia countryside to end in Purcellville. It passes through Falls Church, Vienna, Reston and Herndon before reaching Leesburg. While all this suburban development keeps it from being a truly rural trail in many sections, it also provides opportunities for refreshments and supplies.

Although the trail is well marked, there are many road crossings that require you to slow down and use extra caution. It is also a heavily used trail, and cyclists need to watch for walkers and children. The trail is not well shaded, and you may feel uncomfortably warm on a hot day.

Access to the trail via Metro is easiest from the Dunn Loring station. Head north on Gallows Rd. to join the trail just after S. Park St.

Bikes on Metro

You must acquire a bike-on-rail permit in order to take your bike on Metro trains. The permit ($15 in 1991) is good for five years and allows you to have your bike on the trains on weekends, most holidays, and weekdays after 7 p.m. In addition, you must attend a 30 minute class and pass a simple test to get the permit. These sessions are held at Metro's headquarters, 600 5th St. N.W. Call (202) 962-1116 for times and more information.

Once you have the necessary paperwork, a bike/train combination can work well for an evening ride or a one-way day ride out Rock Creek Park. There is also a book available from The Washington Area Bicyclist Association titled 'Bike Rides from Metro Stations' that lays out 14 rides that are easily accessible from the Metro.

Museums and Monuments on the Mall

Here are just some of the sights and places of interest in the center of D.C. There are lots more tucked away in the downtown area, and more still in the city's outlying areas. Many are accessible by bike, like the National Zoo in Rock Creek Park. The places listed here are all close to the National Monuments route detailed on Map 8 (page 81).

A *Lincoln Memorial.* Open daily 8a.m.-midnight

B *Dept. of State.* Tours by reservation 647-3241

C *Vietnam Veterans Memorial.* Open 24 hours.

D *F.B.I. Building.* 1-hour tours M-F 8:45-4:15

E *White House.* Tours Tu.-Sa. 10a.m.-noon.

F *Bureau of Engraving & Printing.* Tours M-F 9-2

G *Washington Monument.* Open daily.

H *Jefferson Memorial.* Open 8a.m.-midnight

I *Nat'l Mus. of American History.* Daily 10-5:30.

J *Nat'l Mus. of Natural History.* Daily 10-5:30.

K	*National Archives.* Daily 10-5:30 (later in sum.).
L	*Nat'l Gallery of Art.* M-Sa 10-5/Su noon-9.
M	*Nat'l Gallery of Art - East Wing.* Same as L.
N	*U.S. Capitol.* Open daily 9-4:30; tours 9-3:45.
O	*Senate Office Buildings.*
P	*Supreme Court.* Open M-F 9-4:30.
Q	*Library of Congress.* Tours M-F 9-4.
R	*House Office Buildings.*
S	*Air & Space Mus.* Daily 10-5:30 (later in sum.).
T	*Hirshhorn Mus. and Sculpture Grdn.* 10-5:30.
U	*Arts and Industries Bldg.* Open daily 10-5:30.
V	*Smithsonian Institution.* Visitor Info. 10-530.
W	*Sackler Gallery/Mus. African Art.* Daily 10-5:30.
X	*Freer Gallery of Art.*
Y	*U.S. Botanic Garden.* 9-9 summer/9-5 other.

165

Bridge Crossings

The sketch maps below illustrate how to use bike paths to negotiate two of the bridges that cross the Potomac River. Maps 8 and 9 use one or both of these bridges. These maps are adapted from "Getting Around Washington by Bicycle," published by the D.C. Dept. of Transportation. A complete set of bridge maps is included in that guide, along with directions and special cautions.

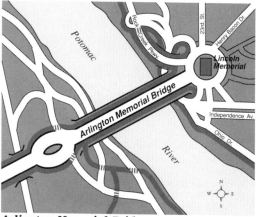

Arlington Memorial Bridge

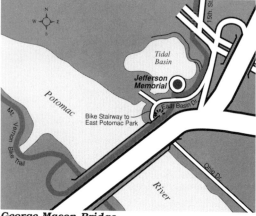

George Mason Bridge

Cycling Information

Bicycle riding in the city and in the country is fun, and will be safer when common sense and basic safety rules are followed. Knowing the rules of the road, developing good riding skills, maintaining a properly equipped bicycle and matching a route to your fitness and skill level will add up to many miles of pleasurable cycle touring. Most of the following safety tips and graphics are reprinted with permission from City of Portland and City of Eugene, Oregon, publications.

Safety tips

In general:
- **Be predictable.** Ride so drivers can see you and predict your movements. The rules in the driver's manual also apply to bicyclists.
- **Be alert.** Ride defensively and expect the unexpected. No matter who is at fault in an accident, the bicyclist loses.
- **Be equipped.** You will ride easier and safer if you and your bike have proper equipment.
- **Wear a helmet.** A hard shell helmet, meeting ANSI or Snell performance standards, is an essential element in your safety program.

Country riding:
- Ride single file and keep to the right when vehicles are approaching from behind and on sections of road with poor visibility.
- Slow down for gravel, sand, wet leaves, potholes, and other poor pavement conditions.
- Watch for dogs — dismount and place your bike between you and the dog if necessary.
- Be prepared for the air turbulence caused by fast moving vehicles or large trucks.
- Treat railroad crossings with respect. Cross perpendicular to the tracks and assure yourself that it is clear and safe before making the crossing.

In traffic:

There are both common sense and legal rules to follow when you are riding your bike in traffic. The following are some basic guidelines for safe cycling.

Obey traffic signs, signals, and laws. Bicyclists must drive like motorists if they are to be taken seriously by motorists.

Never ride against traffic. Motorists are not looking for bicyclists riding against traffic on the wrong side of the road.

Scan the road around you. Keep your eyes roving constantly for cars, pebbles, grates, etc. Learn to look back over your shoulder without swerving.

Use a bike route. Use bike lanes when you can. If a bike lane is not close by, keep up with traffic on narrow, busy streets, or find a quieter street.

Do not pass on the right. On streets without bike lanes, do not overtake an automobile when approaching an intersection or when the automobile is signalling for a turn.

Follow lane markings. Do not turn left from the right lane. Do not go straight in a lane marked for right turn only.

Observe dismount signs. Where requested, dismount and walk your bike.

Choose the best way to turn left.
Either signal, move into the left lane, and turn left, or ride straight to the far crosswalk, and walk your bike across.

Ride in the middle of lane in slow traffic. Get in the middle of the lane at busy intersections and when you are moving at the same speed as traffic.

You may leave a bike lane.
When hazards or obstructions block a bike lane or you are afraid a motorist might turn across your path, you may merge into the adjacent auto lane for safety.

Use lights at night. The law requires a strong headlight and rear reflector or taillight at night or when visibility is poor. Wear light colored clothes with reflective tape for extra protection.

Ride on sidewalks only where permitted. Pedestrians have the right of way. Give them audible warning when you pass. Use extra caution when crossing driveways and intersections.

Ride with both hands ready to brake. Be prepared for quick stops, and in rain allow three times the normal braking distance.

Use hand signals. Hand signals tell motorists what you intend to do. Signal as a matter of law, of courtesy, and of self-protection.

169

Bicycle maintenance

Your bicycle requires periodic inspection and maintenance to keep it running reliably and safely. Several good books are available at bike shops, bookstores and libraries, and bicycle maintenance and repair classes are sometimes offered through the cities and schools.

Here are just a few maintenance pointers:

- Regularly lubricate your bike with the correct type of lubricant.
- Brakes should be checked and adjusted if necessary. Brake shoes should be about one-eighth inch from the rim.
- The chain should be lubricated and clean, and the gears properly adjusted.
- Tires should be fully inflated.
- The frame and attachments should be tight.
- Seat and handlebars should be adjusted correctly for you.

Equipment

Since most of the routes in this book will lead you some distance from home, it is wise to carry at least a basic tool kit with you whenever you are on your bike. Your tool kit should include at least the following items:
- tire repair kit
- tire irons
- pump
- tube valve tool (if not part of valve cap)
- small crescent wrench
- screwdriver

In addition, it may be useful to have:
- spoke wrench
- pliers
- oil
- tape
- allen wrenches
- freewheel remover

Spare parts that can come in handy include:
- cables for derailleur and brakes
- tube
- brake shoes (2)
- spokes (3)

Almost all of these tools and parts will fit into a small seat or handlebar bag, and with them you can tackle just about any problem not requiring a bicycle shop or expert attention.

Clothing

Wearing the right clothes and being prepared for adverse weather conditions will allow you to pedal merrily through varying weather patterns. Consider including these items in your riding wardrobe:

- a hat (in addition to your helmet)
- rain jacket or cape
- rain pants
- pant leg clips
- riding gloves
- sunglasses
- thermal tights and shirt
- riding shorts
- additional layers of clothing

Fitness

One of the most pleasant side effects of touring by cycle or by foot is, of course, the opportunity to raise your general level of fitness. It is recommended that you get a physical examination and discuss a fitness program and activity with your doctor. For the casual daytripper and serious athlete alike, exercise should not be debilitating. Pace yourself, enjoy your activity, and plan your outings to accommodate your fitness level.

Tips:

- Go slowly at first; be patient; and always warm up before a session and cool down afterward.

- Progress at your own rate and try to infuse a long term and consistent outlook into your activity.

- Look for variety in your exercise - both in activity and location.

- Develop a total fitness program that targets strength, aerobic capacity, and flexibility.

- Measure the amount of exercise you are getting in terms of time and intensity rather than just miles covered.

- Learn to pace yourself so that your energy resources are parceled out evenly over the course of the activity you have planned.

- Invest in clothing and equipment that matches your intensity and seriousness, and that adds to your comfort and enjoyment of the activity.

Calorie charts

These are some very approximate figures for calculating calories burned during different types of activities. The numbers inside the grey shaded area show the calories burned per minute for that activity.

Walking

Speed (mph)	Body Weight		
	120 lb	160lb	200lb
2	3	4	4
3	4	5	6
4	5	6	8
5	8	10	13

Running

Pace (min/mi.)	Body Weight		
	120 lb	160lb	200lb
11:30	7	10	12
9:00	10	14	18
8:00	11	15	19
7:00	12	16	21
6:00	14	18	23

Cycling

Speed (mph)	Calories per minute
5	2
10	5
15	10
20	17

More Cycling Guides
from
Terragraphics

Touring New England by Bicycle
New England has long been a favorite destination for a cycling vacation. This guide describes one- to five-day loops throughout the region for all levels of cyclists. Complete information, from spectacular 3-D topographical maps to mileage logs to accommodations, is presented for each route. Whether you are looking for a casual one-day jaunt or an inn-to-inn odyssey on the picturesque backroads of New England, you'll find rides that have been carefully planned by cyclists who have spent years touring here.
$10.95   ISBN 0-944376-08-8

Touring the San Francisco Bay Area by Bicycle
This book offers cyclists 34 rides in the region. Along with these selected loops, maps show hundreds of miles of good cycling roads for an area stretching from northern Marin County all the way to Santa Cruz. The routes included are as varied as the topography and weather of the Bay Area.
$10.95   ISBN 0-944376-05-3

Touring California's Wine Country by Bicycle
These California regions are known worldwide for the quality and variety of their wines. The 34 routes in this guidebook take into account wine tasting opportunities, enjoying the countryside, and getting a good workout. Features rides in Napa, Sonoma, Sierra foothill, Central Valley, and Coast regions.
$10.95   ISBN 0-944376-06-1

(continued)

Touring the Islands

Bicycling in the San Juan, Gulf and Vancouver Islands

This island group annually attracts thousands of cyclists - and for good reason. Country roads, spectacular scenery, ferry rides, and the easy-going atmosphere add up to a great cycling vacation. Twelve islands and the northwest Olympic Peninsula can accommodate from a one-day to a multi-week trip over a variety of terrain.

$10.95   ISBN 0-944376-01-0

Touring Seattle by Bicycle

Thirty-three rides covering a large portion of the Puget Sound area are included. Routes range in character from downtown urban to island farmland. A variety of ride lengths and topography makes this book useful to both novice and expert cyclists. Seattle area riders made this book a regional bestseller in 1989, and will find it a valuable tool for years to come.

$10.95   ISBN 0-944376-02-9

Terragraphics books are distributed by
Ten Speed Press.

Ask for them at your favorite bookstore

-or-

Order direct from Ten Speed Press. Please include $1.25 shipping and handling for the first book, and 50 cents for each additional book. California residents include local sales tax. Write for our free complete catalog of over 400 books and tapes.

TEN SPEED PRESS
Box 7123
Berkeley, California 94707